The Indian *Slow* Cooker

The Indian *Slow Cooker*

A SURREY BOOK • AGATE • CHICAGO

50 HEALTHY, EASY, AUTHENTIC RECIPES   *Anupy Singla*

Printed in China

All photographs copyright © 2010 Brave New Pictures, Inc.

Design by Brandtner Design.

Library of Congress Cataloging-in-Publication Data

Singla, Anupy.
The Indian slow cooker / by Anupy Singla.
    p. cm.
Includes index.
Summary: "Over fifty recipes for preparing Indian food in the slow cooker"--Provided by publisher.
ISBN-13: 978-1-57284-111-6 (pbk.)
ISBN-10: 1-57284-111-7 (pbk.)
1. Electric cookery, Slow. 2. Cookery, Indic. I. Title.
TX827.S5355 2010
641.5'884--dc22

                            2010012820

14 15 16 17   15 14 13 12 11 10 9

Surrey Books is an imprint of Agate Publishing. Agate books are available in bulk at discount prices. For more information, go to agatepublishing.com.

Mom, here is your book.

Contents

Acknowledgments

THIS BOOK IS A TRUE FAMILY EFFORT.

The most credit goes to Veena Singla, my incredibly patient mother, who has written her own cookbook ten times over during the course of the last two decades. Hers was handwritten on index cards and small slips of paper that she would steadfastly and eagerly hand to me through my various stages of life and work, first as an aide on Capitol Hill, then as a graduate student in Hawaii, and still later as a mother myself trying to balance work, kids, and a hungry husband. Mom, I'm writing this for us and to tell you how much I appreciate your persistence and desire to teach your children that cooking can be easy, nutritious, and Indian.

I also want to thank my father, who often showed so much enthusiasm for this project that he kept me on the phone for hours at a time, going over one recipe after another. Dad, it's your love of spicy, authentic Indian food that makes these recipes a representation of everything that is important to our family. You know that Babaji is responsible for all of this. After all, he's the one who gave me my first cooking lesson.

I was also blessed to have a mother-in-law who uses a slow cooker and a father-in-law always willing to taste test. Mattu Massi and Nisha Mamiji, we combined your years living in India with my Indian-American outlook to create unique recipes that are still true to their roots. It was so much fun to exchange recipes with you, and I know this project will connect us in a way we never thought possible.

A huge thank you to my husband and children, who patiently let me experiment on them every step of the way. Granted, I sometimes wonder how I ever finished a book with so many needs to fulfill throughout my day (from bouts of crying, to fighting, to dead fish). But, I have to say, you all helped me realize that the craziness was worth it.

Neha—my older and more organized one—you are the best agent I've ever had. And affordable: You only asked for a quarter per book in return and sold this book to all of your kindergarten classmates and teachers while it was still a mere idea. I learn from your steadfast drive and ambition every day.

Aria, you are hands down the best taste tester anyone could hope for. My younger one, at four years old, would leave Dora, SpongeBob, and Tom and Jerry (her absolute favorite) by the wayside as soon as she saw I was cooking. Aria, you were brave enough to try anything, from fresh spinach to raw garlic. I love you and your amazing spirit.

Sandeep—what can I say? You love to eat. Thank god you're obsessed with raw onions, too! We couldn't have done better.

The first person outside my family I approached about this book was Donna Pierce, at the time assistant food editor and test kitchen director for the *Chicago Tribune*'s food section. I cold-called you, asking for help, and you were nothing but open and encouraging. For that, I thank you wholeheartedly. You've been a voice in the back of my head all through this process.

A huge thank you to all of my amazing taste testers, many of whom I met randomly along the way and who meekly responded "yes" when this persistent stranger asked, "Do you like Indian food?" I figured, who could resist free food? Thank goodness you were all up to the challenge. You made my book better with your honest and thoughtful feedback. And, a big thank you to the folks at Peet's Coffee and Tea on North Avenue in Chicago, who let me sit and write for hours at a time.

Many thanks to my brilliant photographers Dave and Gregg and food stylist Kathy, whose enthusiasm for this project clearly shows through their mouth-watering images. Twenty dishes in two days with two sick kids—we still did it!

I would be remiss if I forgot to thank my fellow "victims" in boot camp at the East Bank Club. Through this class, I culled many a writing opportunity—even this book. It was Amy who introduced me to Janet Fuller, the food editor at the *Chicago Sun-Times*. As soon as I told Janet about my book idea, she put me in touch with my now publisher, Doug Seibold, and the rest is history.

My most sincere thank you goes to Doug. Without your leap of faith, this book would never have existed. You took me on, though this was my first book project. I will never forget the help and the guidance!

Introduction

MY PARENTS MOVED TO AMERICA WHEN I WAS THREE, and after a series of moves, we ended up in King of Prussia, Pennsylvania. Growing up, I ate Indian food almost every day (except for those bouts of boardwalk fries and Steak-umms). I spent many summers in India, watching my paternal grandmother and others in her village make many of the recipes in this book. There, they mash spices by hand and toil over hot clay stoves for hours at a time. They also use pressure cookers, which are fast but often intimidating.

As a television reporter and a writer, I just didn't have the luxury of extra time in my day (who does?), but I was determined to find ways to produce traditional Indian flavors without all the work. Don't get me wrong, some grinding and chopping is still involved in these recipes. But, with the right tools, even those tasks are not complicated. You just have to know which spices and kitchen appliances to have on hand. This book will spell it out for you.

My mother was a typical immigrant to this country: busy with work, but well versed on how to stock our kitchen with the appropriate spices and utensils to make the foods that she and my father grew up eating. But even Mom grew a little weary of tending to dish after dish on the stovetop.

My mom was first introduced to the slow cooker in the 1970s by a coworker. It was the first time she'd ever heard of one, as they didn't exist in India back then. Mom says she began by cooking soups but then began to experiment with Indian food. She became hooked when she realized it saved hours of her time without sacrificing taste.

There are hundreds of Indian cookbooks out there and even more books on slow cooking. But never has one put the two concepts together—until now.

Indian food traditionalists will likely raise an eyebrow. Most Indian dishes are based on making a *tardka*—infusing extremely hot oil with whole and ground spices to season your dish. Usually, after a curried dish is prepared, oil or *ghee* is heated in a separate frying pan. Just as the oil begins to smoke a bit, cumin or mustard seeds and other whole spices are added, along with chopped or sliced onions, ginger, and garlic. This mixture is then added to the prepared dish just before serving, enhancing its flavor. Some of my friends who use slow cookers still finish off their dishes with a fried *tardka*.

After much experimentation, I've discovered that for most dishes you can eliminate this step without sacrificing taste, reducing the hands-on prep process to a mere twenty-minute affair and eliminating virtually all fat. I have included the *tardka* process in a few dishes that I believe still need it—especially those that use mustard or fenugreek seeds, as without the hot oil the seeds won't pop or roast to the right flavor.

Hours of stewing in a slow cooker enables spices to infuse your dishes. Lentils and beans cook to perfection, breaking down just to the point of creaminess without the use of crutches like cream, which just add unnecessary calories and unhealthy fat. You can also forgo canned beans for their dried counterparts, which cook better. The canned beans have already expanded and don't break down in the same manner as the dried during the cooking process. This is great news for the cook on a budget, because dried beans are cheaper and can be purchased in bulk.

It is also great news for Indians across the globe suffering from heart disease and/or diabetes. The latest research shows that Asian Indians have one of the highest rates of heart disease in the world because of possible genetic abnormalities. If you are of South Asian decent, you don't need a statistic for proof. All you have to do is look at your own family. In mine, I've lost three dear uncles (*mamajis*) to heart disease. My father and father-in-law fight this daily battle as well. My recipes can add more oil-free, nonfat, even vegan options to the dinner table. Spicy, flavorful, and authentic cuisine doesn't have to be loaded with unhealthy oils and fats. My book will prove it to every person in your life that suffers from these illnesses.

There's also variety in this book. I've taken the basic Indian vegetarian dishes, most of which I've always made in the slow cooker, and expanded them to include meat and desserts. Your family will love the flavor. If they don't care for the spiciness of traditional Indian food, remember that you can always modify the amount of heat and salt according to your taste. I often cook a dish with green chiles and red chile powder in my large slow cooker for my husband and older daughter and simultaneously make the exact same dish without chiles in my mini slow cooker for our younger daughter.

There is nothing healthier to feed your family than beans and lentils. Add the flavor of authentic spices like cumin and turmeric to the health benefits, and you have recipes that you'll make for years to come. With the help of my mother and mother-in-law, I've developed great-tasting recipes that require mere minutes of prep time. They are all based on traditional family recipes that have been handed down through generations—from my grandparents, to my own parents, and now from me to my two girls and to you.

Welcome to the family!

Getting Started

"The advantage of Indian slow cooking is that it is scalable ... virtually every recipe can be cut in half or by a third, and its taste and look will parallel the original recipe."

What in the World Is a Slow Cooker? Why Should I Use One?

MY MOTHER GAVE ME MY OWN SLOW COOKER DURING MY FRESHMAN YEAR of college. Little did I know that I was part of a global trend.

Since the Rival Company rolled out the first slow cooker, the Crock-Pot, in 1971, they have sold over 100 million of the various models they offer. These days, Rival corners about 85 percent of the slow cooker market with at least 15 different models and sizes, but there are now many other brands from which to choose. Some helpful options to look for include automatic timers, locks to keep your slow cooker tightly closed while transporting food, stainless steel inserts, and inserts that can safely sit on a stovetop to brown meats before slow cooking.

I tested my recipes in the 5-quart round Rival Crock-Pot (without a timer). My mother always used this brand, so I naturally gravitated toward it. I needed four of them to tackle several recipes at one time, so the reasonable price point made sense. Though some of the larger Rival slow cookers are criticized for cooking at too high a temperature on the high setting and burning food, I didn't have this issue with this particular model. The one thing I didn't like was that it didn't have an indicator light to show that it was on. At times, I would have to wait for it to heat up to ensure that food was cooking.

I recommend this size slow cooker for any family that likes leftovers and for party cooking. The lid jiggles a little bit during cooking, but the moisture does not escape and food cooks evenly.

If you don't like a ton of leftovers and are newer to slow cooker recipes, start with a 3½ quart. This is the size I used when I scaled down my recipes. I tried the Rival in this size but found that water seeped out from the sides of the lid during cooking, drying out my food. I invested a little more and purchased a Cuisinart in this size with an automatic timer. I was very happy with the appliance, which allowed me to program the number of hours I needed to cook and just leave. Once the cooking time ended, the slow cooker would automatically put the dish on warm until I turned it off.

Various sizes of slow cookers are available, so you may want to experiment to find the right size for you and your family. Obviously, it would have been next to impossible to test all my recipes in all the brands and sizes available. Instead, I focused on testing my recipes in a 5-quart slow cooker. If you want to make the lentil and bean recipes in a 4-quart slow cooker, just reduce the legume by a cup and also reduce the corresponding amount of water. For example, if a recipe calls for 3 cups of lentils and 12 cups of water, reduce to 2 cups of lentils and 8 cups of water. Pare back the other ingredients slightly.

I've also tested all my recipes in a 3½ quart slow cooker, which is ideal for smaller family meals or if you're cooking for one. The cooking time remains the same.

Make sure the slow cooker is at least half full to avoid burning, and never fill it completely to the top to avoid spills. You'll need to experiment a little if you use a different cooker.

The advantage of Indian slow cooking is that it is scalable, which helps when testing different sized slow cookers. Virtually every recipe can be cut in half or a third, and its taste and look will parallel the original recipe. Or, if you would like to cook an even larger amount, increase the proportions by a third or half. Just realize that you may need to tweak water amounts and heating times according to the brand and size of the slow cooker you use.

Keep in mind that the smallest slow cookers on the market usually don't have different heating levels and will not cook beans as well as a cooker that allows you to cook on high. For the best results, select a slow cooker with at least two heat levels.

The one thing that most slow cookers have in common, regardless of the brand, is their cooking mechanism. A thick insert made of stoneware sits inside a metal casing, and the electrical heating elements in this casing carry the heat up and around the stoneware insert, where the food cooks. This provides an even, low, moist heat. (Companies are also starting to make inserts out of stainless steel.) The slow cooker basically keeps food constantly simmering at the lowest possible temperature for longer periods of time. Because there is no open heating surface or flame, you can safely turn on your slow cooker and leave.

Slow cookers use little electricity. They usually have a low and high setting. On low, they use about the same amount of energy as a 75-watt light bulb, and on high, they use less than 300 watts. It takes much less electricity to use a slow cooker than a conventional gas or electric oven.

Slow cookers are safe to use when you're not at home. Most medium to large slow cookers come with two settings: low and high. Foods will cook more quickly on the high setting, but if you will be out all day or are using less-tender cuts of meat, put the setting on low. A good trick is to start the cooker on high for an hour or so while you get ready in the morning, and then turn it to low before you leave for work. Most of the small-sized slow cookers only have a low setting. This safety mechanism is primarily due to the size of the contraption. Be sure to clear the area around your apparatus when it is on, so that nothing touches it.

Food cooked in a slow cooker is safe. In a slow cooker, food cooks more slowly and at a lower temperature than it would on the stovetop or in the oven. However, the lengthy cooking time, the heat coming from all directions, and the concentrated steam held inside the appliance all work to destroy bacteria and keep food safe. According to the Food and Drug Administration, bacteria thrive at temperatures between 40 degrees and 140 degrees Fahrenheit. If you're worried about the low start temperatures, cook on high for a few hours before switching to low. In general, food-borne bacteria are more of a concern with meat dishes.

If your electricity shuts off during the cooking process and you're unable to refrigerate the food immediately, for safety reasons it's best to discard the contents and start over. Generally, the slow cooker is not adequate to reheat food. They just can't be brought up to a sufficient temperature quickly enough. Stick to the stovetop or microwave for reheating.

Don't put frozen foods in your slow cooker. It takes too long to boost the heat of foods that are frozen in a slow cooker. The best way to cook with meats and vegetables that are frozen is to first defrost them completely. In a few recipes, I add a small amount of frozen peas at the end of the cooking process, which doesn't affect cooking times.

Don't overfill or under fill your slow cooker. In order to cook your food safely and prevent burning your appliance, your slow cooker should be filled between half and three-quarters full.

Don't confuse a slow cooker with a pressure cooker. A pressure cooker locks in steam and heat so that it can cook food within minutes. If you are South Asian, your mother probably grew up using pressure cookers. These appliances have evolved and have become safer, but the buildup of steam to the point of bursting has created an aura of danger around pressure cookers that many cannot overcome—myself included. To boot, you aren't likely to obtain the same depth of taste with a pressure cooker as you can with a slow cooker, which allows dishes to stew and flavors to meld for hours.

Take care of your slow cooker. Never submerge the base of the slow cooker in water. Instead, wait for it to cool down and then clean it gently with a damp cloth. The ceramic cooking vessel that fits in the base can be washed liberally in a sink with hot, soapy water and should be thoroughly cleaned after each use.

Can these recipes be made on the stovetop? Absolutely. Just keep in mind that when cooking on the stove, you'll use a quarter more water because liquids evaporate. So, if a slow cooker recipe requires 4 cups of water, use 5 cups when making it on the stovetop. Also, though you can keep your pot at a low simmer on the stovetop, you still always want to keep an eye on it to prevent drying and burning. If food—especially beans and other legumes—starts to dry out, just add more water and continue to cook.

The rule in the land of slow cookers is usually never to open the lid while cooking for fear of losing critical heat and slowing down the cooking process. This may be true, but I have a tough time following the rules myself. Also, there are some dishes, such as Curried Spinach with Homemade Cheese (*Palak Paneer*), that need to be stirred during cooking. Know that the cooking times cited in my recipes reflect my inability to keep the lid shut, so to speak. Just do your best to limit peeking. A good rule-of-thumb is to add about 5 minutes of cooking time for every time you lift the lid.

Never try to heat an empty slow cooker, as the insert can crack and be damaged. If you want to preheat, fill the cooker with water and turn on high.

Don't use an extension cord with a slow cooker. It's best to plug directly into an outlet.

Why Indian?

WHEN YOU THINK OF INDIAN FOOD, WHAT COMES TO MIND? BE HONEST. Are you concerned that you'll have to invest in dozens upon dozens of unfamiliar spices? That you'll be in the kitchen for hours preparing just one meal? That you'll need layer upon layer of creams and unhealthy oils, or—worse yet—that incredibly spicy food will keep you in the bathroom for hours the next day? If you are thinking all of these things, don't worry— you're not alone. Unfortunately, this is the image of Indian food in America.

Most Indian restaurants have helped create this image. The food they offer is an interpretation of classic North Indian—Punjabi—cooking. Traditionally, Punjabis from India and Pakistan have been pivotal in opening and running successful restaurants overseas.

The food that these restaurants offer, however, is not the food that I grew up with. It is often dripping with oils or laden with unhealthy cream. My husband and I avoid buffets like the plague for fear of all the unhealthy fats. I did have lunch at a buffet one day and looked down at my plate in amazement. I had three distinct dishes, in theory and name, on my plate, but in the end they all tasted like the same dish. Why? Because after preparing them, the cooks dumped cream in every dish, from the black lentils, to the cheese and peas, to the mixed veggies. This is what they think customers want!

If the food is good at an Indian restaurant, the price is unnerving. I still remember one of the first Indian restaurants that opened in Philadelphia. My parents and I went, thrilled that our cuisine was finally represented. My father, though, just couldn't get past the tiny bowl of curried chickpeas they brought out. It was barely enough for one person, let alone three adults. They charged us about $8.00, which was a lot in the 1980s.

The cost of *dal* makes us laugh the most. I'm not sure why a dish of lentils and veggies —and, okay, a touch of cream—is sometimes priced as high as $12.00, when the main ingredient costs mere pennies per serving. In fact, lentils are what poor workers living and working on the streets of India eat, because it's the cheapest and most nutritious food around. So, why are we paying all this money for food that is often unhealthy and nontraditional?

The answer is that most people just don't know any better. They don't realize that Indian food is easy to make or that it's incredibly varied. You don't have to limit yourself to the dishes you find in restaurants. You can put a South Indian slant on a dish simply by substituting mustard seeds for cumin or try a Goan-inspired dish by using coconut milk. The possibilities are endless.

If you don't believe me, read on.

Indian Spices 101

MOST PEOPLE ARE AFRAID TO COOK INDIAN FOOD BECAUSE THEY mistakenly believe that they need to have complicated spices on hand. I'm here to say "nonsense!" to that.

Yes, there are many spices out there. But to start cooking the Indian dishes most commonly found on restaurant menus, you only need a few key spices, some of which you may already have in your cupboard. To make most North Indian dishes, start by investing in cumin seeds, black or brown mustard seeds, ground coriander, turmeric powder, red chile powder, black

MASALA DABBA

1. *Red Chile Powder*
2. *Ground Coriander*
3. *Black Mustard Seeds*
4. *Turmeric Powder*
5. *Black Salt/Kala Namak*
6. Garam Masala
7. *Cumin Seeds*

salt, and *garam masala.* I also like to keep regular table salt, kosher salt, and sea salt on hand for general flavoring.

All of the above spices can be found at any Indian grocery store. Most are also now available at well-stocked grocers like Whole Foods Market. If your local grocery store doesn't have the spices you need, then check on the Internet. There are many online sites now that sell Indian spices.

Storing and dispensing these spices will be incredibly simple if you invest in what's known among Indians as a *masala dabba.* This spice box is one of the quintessential tools in the Indian kitchen: a simple, stainless steel box. Round in shape, it hold seven smaller bowls—small enough to fit into the palm of your hand—that hold small amounts of the seven essential spices needed for Indian cooking.

The best feature of this container is that the small bowls can be removed so that you can dole out spices right over any dish you are making. A tiny spoon inside the box helps get the measurements just right. The *dabba* can fit into most kitchen drawers and ensures that spices are readily available to add to oil as it heats up on the stovetop. Timing is essential to getting Indian food just right, and it's difficult to get the timing down if you are fumbling in cupboards and with various containers as you cook. What's nice about Indian slow cooker cooking is that it's less sensitive to timing than on the stovetop. Nonetheless, I still recommend purchasing a *masala dabba.* If you purchase more than one, each can be used to store the most-used spices for a particular region in India. You can even make one box for baking spices and another for Italian, or one for oatmeal toppings. The possibilities are endless.

The spices you use will vary depending on the region of India from which the dish originates. I am from Punjab, so much of what I've presented in this book is from North India, though I've also included some South Indian and Goan recipes. Most Indian restaurants offer North Indian cuisine, so the dishes you're most used to eating, from *Palak Paneer* to Chicken Curry, are probably represented in this cookbook.

You will have the best luck cooking Indian food if you buy most of your spices whole and in small quantities. Ground, they have a shorter shelf life, so don't buy ground spices in large quantities unless you know you'll go through them quickly. I do purchase turmeric and red chile in powder form because it's difficult to grind these two spices. Red chile can irritate the eyes, and it's tough to find turmeric in its whole form.

Invest in a basic coffee grinder, and reserve it only for grinding whole spices. Grinding spices takes seconds. Put them in the grinder, push down for a few seconds, and they're ready to use. As long as the grinder stays dry, it only needs to be washed about once a month.

Some recipes call for roasting spices. Don't be intimidated. Think of it as a way to get double duty from your spices. Use a dry, shallow pan—one that has no water in it or any remnants of oil. Put your spice in the pan and heat on medium-low heat for a few minutes, until browned. Stay close by as the spice cooks and shake the pan a few times to ensure it doesn't burn. When the spice has browned, immediately transfer it to a room-temperature container to cool for about 10 minutes. If you grind roasted spices while they are hot, they will release moisture and will cake at the bottom of your grinder. If this happens, just scrape out your spice and add to your dish.

The key to keeping your spices fresh is to keep moisture away from the box in which you store your spices. The spoon you use to dispense the spices should be kept dry and clean. If you wash your containers, make sure they are completely dry before you refill them. And never use a spoon that was used for something else before but now looks dry. Spices are sensitive to contamination and you want to be as cautious as possible.

Below is a list of the spices used in all of the recipes in this book with a brief explanation on the taste of each and why it's used. Start slow, with the most basic and essential spices—you can always add later.

Amla: This tiny fruit is an Indian gooseberry, which is extremely tart and the richest natural source of vitamin C. It's a delicious addition to one of my chickpea dishes. Some soak *amla* in hot water and have it as a health drink in the morning. You'll find it at an Indian grocery store. I recommend buying it unsalted, dried, and sliced rather than shredded.

I'm proud to say most of the *amla* we use comes right from my mom's childhood home in Chandigarh, India. There is one tree in the backyard that gives off so much fruit that my aunt sells it to the local market and distributes it to visiting family members.

Asafetida powder (hing): This is not the most pleasant-smelling ingredient, but it helps digestion when it is added to food in very small pinches. The smell is quite strong, so store it in an airtight, sealed container so the smell doesn't permeate the entire cupboard. One way to eliminate the smell is to put it in heated oil, butter, or *ghee*.

Most of the recipes in this book don't include *hing*, but if you are extra sensitive to any spice, just heat some up on the stovetop and add it toward the end of cooking.

Bay leaf (Indian): Indian bay leaves look like their European counterpart, but they have more of a cinnamon flavor. You can find them in most Indian grocery stores, but if you don't have them, you can substitute European bay leaves.

Big/Black cardamom (bardi elaichi): This is a big, dark, woody version of the small, green cardamom we are all used to seeing. It tastes fantastic in my black chickpea curry. It's also a healer when you have a cold. Just crush it gently and add it into the boiling water when you make *chai*, and you should be on your way to feeling better. It tastes great in rice *palau* as well.

Black salt (kala namak): This is my favorite Indian spice. It's actually a rock salt that's somewhat pinkish in color. It has a tangy taste and smell and enhances the taste of any dish in which you use it. In North India, it is used to flavor snacks, salads, and yogurt. A little of this spice goes a long way, so be careful to use small amounts until you get the spicing just right.

Cardamom (green and white) (hari elaichi): Cardamom is the flavor behind Indian tea and many other dishes, including well-spiced basmati rice, meat stews, and desserts such as *kheer*. The seeds are ground to make cardamom powder and are a great addition to mango smoothies. Cardamom is also a great breath freshener. My mother carries whole pods around in her purse and pulls some out to chew on after eating strong Indian food or raw onions. The green ones are most common in Indian cooking. The white, used in Europe for baking, is merely a green cardamom pod bleached white with sulfur dioxide.

Carom seeds (ajwain, ajowan): This small seed has a very pungent flavor and smell. It looks like cumin (*jeera*) and is used in Indian breads like *parantha* and in snacks. I use a pinch of it in the Kitchari, as it has healing properties for an upset stomach. Take a teaspoon in hot water with a pinch of salt, and usually your stomachache will disappear.

Caraway seeds (*shyah jeera*): *Shyah* means black, and the reference to *jeera* is because caraway looks like cumin seeds. It adds a special flavor to certain *mughlai* dishes (Pakistani and Indian cuisine influenced by the imperial kitchens of the Mughal Empire) and to my dry black chickpea curry.

Cinnamon sticks (*dalchini*): In India, cinnamon is not reserved for baking but is included in many savory dishes, vegetarian and meat based. But, in the slow cooker, you have to be careful how you use it. After long hours of cooking it will impart a strong flavor and a darker color that are not appealing in certain foods. I use cinnamon sticks for darker lentils but avoid using it in dishes that need to be brighter in color. A dash of ground cinnamon toward the end of cooking can also sometimes do the trick.

CINNAMON STICKS

Cloves (*laung*): Small and black with a bumpy end, this tiny spice packs a strong punch. It's used to spice tea, basmati rice, and many other dishes. Use sparingly, as too much flavor can overpower a dish. Cloves are also used to cure toothaches. Just bite down on one in the area of the ache until the pain subsides.

Coriander seeds/powder (*sabud dhaniya*): Coriander is also known as cilantro. The seeds are round and yellow-green and come from the flowers of the coriander plant. My mother rarely used coriander powder in her cooking, but I've since realized its value in many dishes. It imparts a subtle, unique, lemony flavor. It also imparts more depth to a dish when used along with cumin seeds. Powdered coriander is available in most Indian grocery stores, but the freshest way to get the powder is to grind the seeds in a coffee grinder reserved for spices on an as-needed basis.

Cumin seeds (*jeera*): In North Indian cooking, *jeera* is an essential spice. The seeds smell earthy when heated in oil and impart a strong, characteristically North Indian flavor when used in curries, dried dishes, and rice.

Roasted cumin: This is one of the best-kept secrets in the Indian kitchen. Roasted cumin is essential in most Indian snack foods, yogurt *raitas*, and many other dishes. It's easy to make as well. Just heat a dry pan over medium-high on the stovetop. Place about a tablespoon of cumin seeds in the pan and heat until they turn dark brown, almost black. Be careful not to burn them. Cool and then grind in a coffee grinder reserved for spices, in a mortar and pestle, or with a rolling pin between two paper towels.

Cumin and coriander seeds, roasted: This is a wonderful combination of the nuttier cumin and the lemon-flavored coriander. Mix one tablespoon of each seed in a shallow, dry pan on the stovetop over medium-high heat, and brown, but don't burn. Cool completely and then grind in a coffee grinder reserved for spices or in a mortar and pestle.

Curry leaves: If you haven't had the pleasure of trying curry leaves in your food, you really are missing out. These small, green leaves come from a tree native to India and Sri Lanka and are used predominantly in South Indian cooking. Typically, the leaves are roasted in oil and then added to a dish. Curry leaves are the essential ingredient in *sambhar masala.*

Fennel seeds (*saunf*): Great for digestion, these little green seeds with a licorice-type taste are usually found at the entrance of most Indian restaurants, to be eaten after a meal in small pinches for digestion and freshening the breath. I was excited to find a few dishes that incorporate the seeds fresh and roasted. I also like to include a pinch in my *masala* when making Indian tea. When boiled a few minutes in water, fennel seeds can relieve gas. When my girls were babies I would let them sip cooled spoonfuls of fennel water to help them burp.

Fenugreek seeds/leaves (*methi seeds/leaves*): Small and hard, these seeds are mustard yellow in color. They have a very distinct taste and can be especially bitter when cooked. This bitterness is usually welcome in the dishes in which they are used, such as *khardi* and sweet and sour pumpkin. The key when using these seeds is to cook them just until they have browned. Too little or too much cooking tends to enhance their bitterness.

The green leaves are delicious when used to make Indian breads such as *parantha* and dishes such as chicken curry. They can be purchased fresh or dried. I prefer dried, because they are easier to find and impart a richer flavor.

CURRY LEAVES

CUMIN SEEDS

GROUND CUMIN

ROASTED GROUND CUMIN

FENUGREEK SEEDS

CLOVES

CORIANDER SEEDS

GROUND CORIANDER

BLACK MUSTARD SEEDS

TURMERIC POWDER

BLACK SALT/*KALA NAMAK*

GARAM MASALA

GREEN CARDAMOM

Kokum (*cocum, kokam*): This small, round fruit is native to the western coastal region of Southern India. It's black to dark purple and has a seed inside. The meat is used to add a bit of depth and a unique sweet and salty taste to Southern Indian dishes.

Mango powder (*amchur*): This is a tart, beige powder made from uncooked, dried green mangoes. It is wonderful sprinkled on Indian snack foods and in dishes such as okra, *karela* (bitter gourd), and fried potato. It takes the place of lemon juice or vinegar and is usually used at the end of the cooking process. It's also used to tenderize meat.

Masala: By definition, a *masala* is simply a mixture of ground, roasted spices. There are many *masalas* on the market. You can buy them pre-roasted and ground, or you can purchase whole spices and replicate the blends yourself.

Garam masala: This spice mix is one of the most common in North India. It includes coriander, cumin, cloves, cardamom, black pepper, cinnamon, and nutmeg. You can purchase the spices already ground or buy a packet of all of the above combined but left whole for you to grind later. If you grind them yourself, remember to balance the amount of each spice used. And be careful, as the whole cinnamon can be a little challenging to grind all the way down. Don't be intimidated to go this route though—I've done it and the results are wonderful. In most dishes, the *garam masala* is sprinkled over the food toward the end of cooking, but I prefer to put it in at the beginning along with the other spices.

Chana masala: This spice blend, found at any Indian grocer, has a unique tartness that is essential to my curried chickpea dish. Pomegranate, fenugreek, mustard, and coriander seeds are just a few of the key ingredients.

Chaat masala: This spice mix is tart and ready to use for seasoning snacks called *chaats*. The spices that make this mix unique include asafetida, *amchur* (green mango powder), black salt, cayenne, *ajwain*, cumin, and pepper. *Chaat masala* sprinkled on fruit or veggies enhances their taste and makes a great snack.

Sambhar masala: This is an amazingly fragrant mix of spices that is used to spice a traditional South Indian lentil stew called *sambhar*. The stew is then eaten with *idli* or savory crepes called *dosas*. The spice blend includes lentils, curry leaves, dried chiles, *chana dal*, coriander seeds, cumin seeds, fenugreek seeds, mustard seeds, white poppy seeds, cinnamon sticks, and oil. See page 63 for the recipe.

Mustard seeds (*rai*): These seeds are to South India what cumin seeds are to North India. They come in yellow and brownish-black. The brownish-black seeds are more commonly used. The best way to cook with them is to put them into hot oil and then cover the pan until they pop a bit. Mustard seeds can be used in everything from salads, to lentil stews, to pickles. They can add tartness to a dish when ground to a powder, and they provide a mustard taste when ground to a paste. In South India, they are fried in oil and used in yogurt.

Nigella seeds (*kalonji*): These small black seeds have the combined flavor of onions and black peppers. They are used in North India in pickles and as a decoration for breads such as *naan*.

Red chile powder (*lal mirch*): This red powder made from dried chiles adds color and heat to a dish. Use sparingly for a milder dish, but if you don't mind spicy food, you'll want to be more generous. Cayenne pepper is an acceptable substitute.

Saffron (*kesar*): For decades, saffron was the world's most expensive spice by weight. It's derived from the red, dried stigma of the saffron crocus flower. A little goes a long way, and its musky taste adds depth to savory dishes such as *palau* and sweet dishes such as *kheer*. It's also used for prayer ceremonies and to make a red mark on the forehead as a blessing.

Tamarind (*imlee/imli*): Tamarind trees are easy to spot, with long, beige fruit hanging from their branches. The pods are used to make tamarind, a souring agent used in many Indian dishes, especially those common to South Indian cuisine. Tamarind can be purchased as a block of pulp, which then needs to be boiled down and strained, or as tamarind puree or concentrate.

Turmeric powder (*haldi*): I love *haldi* because it's such a versatile spice. In its whole form, it looks a lot like ginger root, but it's orange/yellow in color on the inside. In my mother's childhood home, they grow it in the backyard, dry it, and grind it into a powder, which they distribute among their large family. It's extremely unusual to find it fresh, but the powder form can now be found almost anywhere

Powdered *haldi* is critical to most Indian dishes. It's also an amazing healer. I add it to hot water with a black tea bag and salt and gargle with the combo to get rid of congestions and coughs. Some studies now indicate the compound curcumin in this amazing spice may help to prevent the onset of Alzheimer's disease. True or not, you can't go wrong by including turmeric in your diet. When you cook with it, be careful not to use too much. A little goes a long way, and the taste can overwhelm a dish.

White salt (*namak*): Indians are pretty salt obsessed. Salt is an amazing flavor enhancer and a key ingredient to really getting the spices in a dish to mix and work together. I only cook with kosher or sea salt, the crystals of which are larger than regular table salt crystals, so you might need to use less when you replicate these recipes. Go ahead and err on the side of caution by adding less than you think you may need—you can always add more salt later. Remember, unless otherwise specified, always use level, and not heaping, teaspoons or tablespoons of salt.

Tools of the Trade

LIKE GETTING SPICES JUST RIGHT, CERTAIN KITCHEN TOOLS MAKE cooking Indian food—especially in a slow cooker—easier. Some you absolutely need, and some you can do without for now but might want to add later.

Slow cookers in different sizes: Ideally, you should have one 4- to 6-quart slow cooker and one 3½-quart slow cooker. The smaller size is especially nice when you don't want to make a huge quantity of food. It also helps when you want to cook a milder version of the same dish for the kids or other spice-sensitive family members. I tested the recipes in this book in a 5-quart medium Rival Crock-Pot and a 3½-quart Cuisinart slow cooker with a timer.

Spice box (*masala dabba*): This traditionally round, stainless steel box comes with up to seven round bowls and small serving spoons. It is ideal for housing your most-used spices. Keep it in a kitchen drawer to pull out as needed. For North Indian cooking, the most important spices to have on hand include whole cumin, mustard and coriander seeds, turmeric powder, red chile powder, green mango powder, and *garam masala*.

Coffee grinder: This small gadget can usually be picked up for under twenty bucks and is worth every penny. It's vital if you plan to grind your own spices. Just be sure to reserve it only for spices and use another grinder for coffee.

Mortar and pestle: This traditional spice grinder requires more effort but is wonderful when you just need to coarsely crush a few spices. We pull it out when making *masala* for Indian tea or just to keep my girls busy while I handle a more involved task.

Hand or immersion blender: Hands down, this is the best $20 investment I've ever made. This long-handled tool with a blade at the bottom enables you to blend and mix a dish without transferring it to another container. Cooked spinach and mustard greens become *saag* in seconds, and cooked peas are blended into soups even faster. You can blend while the slow cooker is still on and continue to cook after. If you don't have an immersion blender, a regular blender will do, but you'll have to take food out of the slow cooker to blend and then transfer it back, which will increase the cooking time.

Food processor: A regular or mini food processor is essential to grind ingredients such as garlic and ginger.

Microplane grater: I have grown to rely on my tiny microplane grater. When I go to conduct cooking demonstrations, I actually keep it in my back pocket. With it, I can quickly grate ginger and garlic instead of chopping it, and I can work on my cutting board or over my slow cooker.

Fresh Ingredients & Pantry Staples

Aata (*roti/parantha* flour): Indians favor this flour, found in Indian grocery stores, for making Indian flat breads such as *roti* and *parantha*. Traditionally, *aata* is made from whole wheat. My mother still remembers her own mother sending out wheat kernels to be ground and used in the kitchen. The wheat used in India is softer than the variety used to make the flours found in most western supermarkets. Over the years, *aata* sold by Indian grocers became a mixture of white and whole-wheat flour. It made for a lighter, fluffier *roti*, but also one that was less healthy. To get the most nutritional benefit out of your homemade Indian bread, purchase *aata* with a label that reads "100 percent whole wheat." If you don't have access to an Indian grocer, any whole-wheat flour will do the trick if combined with an equal amount of all-purpose flour.

Achaar (Indian pickle): Indians adore their pickles, which are nothing like pickles found in the West. Indians pickle everything from mangoes and lemons to large red chile peppers. The fruits and vegetables are preserved in vinegar, brine, or their own juice. The taste can be sweet, spicy, sour, or a combination. These pickles are served on the sides of dishes and eaten in small bites along with bread or rice. The simplest meals sometimes consist of a stack of *rotis* and a delicious piece of *achaar* on the side.

Buttermilk: In many parts of India, buttermilk is eaten after meals in place of yogurt. A by-product of the buttermaking process, it's easier to digest and has a delicious, tangy taste. Some use it to also make *paneer*.

Chile peppers: Using chiles in Indian cooking is not just about adding heat. It's also about adding flavor. Different chiles impart different tastes, and some work better than others in Indian cooking. The smaller the chile, the hotter it's likely to be and the more flavor it will have. The ideal chiles for Indian cooking are the small, green Thai chiles or the slightly longer serrano, which look like long, knobby fingers. The cayenne chile pepper is also a good choice. Avoid the jalapeno pepper because it has a very thick skin that just doesn't work well in Indian cooking. If that's all you can find, go ahead and use it, but be aware that it's not the best choice. Because I love spicy flavors, I've also tried using the super hot habanero and was disappointed. The taste just doesn't work for Indian food, and it's way too spicy to use for everyday cooking. Also remember that most of a chile's heat is found in its seeds. If you want the flavor minus the heat, just cut out the seeds and discard them. Or, use whole chiles in your cooking, just cutting the stems away. This way, you get the amazing flavors without too much spice. Keep that in mind when deciding how many chiles to put into a dish. If you're using bigger, longer chiles you'll want to cut down on the number until you're used to the spiciness. In all my recipes, I've used the Thai chile.

Cilantro (*dhania*): This green, flavorful herb is absolutely essential to Indian cooking. Usually added at the end of cooking, it adds another dimension to the taste of your food. It's optional, but if you use it you can take a dish from perfect to heavenly. It's important to use this ingredient fresh. It can be found in all supermarkets now, especially because it's also commonly used in Mexican cooking. Use the stems along with the leaves.

Coconut: Shredded coconut is used in many South Indian dishes and some North Indian desserts. Ideally, it's best to shred from a fresh coconut, but when fresh is not available, purchase it dried from the store. Most grocery stores carry shredded, unsweetened coconut. Avoid the shredded, sweetened coconut used for baking.

Coconut milk: If you've ever seen a fresh coconut split, you know that they contain a natural liquid. This liquid is not the milk. The milk is actually a sweet, white base derived from cooking the white meat of the coconut. It's used extensively in South Indian and Goan cooking. In the West, this coconut milk is found in a can, in regular and light versions. You can use either in the recipes in this book that call for coconut milk.

Garlic (*lassan*): The power of garlic is amazing. Of course it's a key ingredient in Indian foods. It's also a healer. If you have a cold or a fever, just mince a clove of garlic and swallow with water. You'll be better in a matter of hours. Because I use so much garlic, I usually buy it

already peeled from the supermarket. Just be sure to use it in a timely fashion, as it goes bad faster than whole heads that you have to peel.

Ghee (clarified butter/oil): In India, *ghee*, or clarified butter, is commonly used in all aspects of cooking. It's prized for its ability to be heated to high temperatures without burning and for its aromatic taste and smell. But *ghee* is not the only thing you can use. Many Indian cooks also use vegetable or canola oil. Canola is usually the safest bet, as it has a high tolerance for heat.

My mother used olive oil when I was growing up. I've heard many other Indian cooks warn people off olive oil, saying it has a strong taste that doesn't work well in Indian food. I would disagree. I've never really noticed a difference, but that may be just because I'm now used to eating it. For the purpose of this book, I've stuck with vegetable and canola oils. Feel free to experiment and decide for yourself.

Mustard oil is also used in North and East India, while untoasted sesame and peanut oil is used in the west, and coconut oil is used in the south. These oils all have strong flavors, so experiment first and see what works best for you.

For an extra nutritional boost, add a tablespoon (15 mL) of flax seed oil to any dish or a dash on a hot *roti* before serving for essential omega-3 and -6 fatty acids. Avoid cooking with this oil, as heat will destroy its healthy properties.

Ginger root (Adarak): Ginger root is commonly used in Indian cooking. The freshest is young root with very thin, almost pink skin. I've only found it this way a few times, so look for the more common, thicker-skinned variety. Adding ginger to your dishes adds a flavor and a pop to your food that you can't get any other way. I prefer grated ginger in my recipes, as it adds more flavor with fewer pieces to bite into later. Try peeling a large piece of ginger and freezing it. This makes grating easier.

Gram flour (Besan): If you're serious about Indian cooking, this pale yellow flour is one that you'll want to keep handy. It's made of skinned, split, and ground black chickpeas. I use it in my *khardi* dish, and it's also used for the batter to make *pakoras* (a fried dumpling). It is also used as a thickener and for making breads. You may be able to find *besan* in your local supermarket.

Mint (*pudina*): In North India, unlike other parts of the country, mint is not used a great deal in the dishes themselves, though one or two may include this herb. Mint is primarily ground with spices, sometimes including cilantro, to make a popular green chutney that's eaten along with meals, on many Indian snack foods, and as a sandwich spread. I grew up loving butter and mint chutney sandwiches. Though incredibly simple, you just can't beat the taste.

Onions (*pyaz*): The story goes that I've been eating raw onions since I was three years old. I believe it, because my daughters are the same way: onion obsessed. I love them. I eat them raw. I'm a true Punjabi Indian! Yellow and red onions work best when cooking Indian food. White onions are too sweet for cooking, but they work well in side salads. Onions are essential in most Indian dishes and salads. Once you cook a dish, always top it with a handful of chopped onions. Keep in mind, however, that some communities in India don't cook with onions, garlic, or ginger because of religious and dietary reasons.

Paneer: Homemade cheese is important to most Indian households—especially if they don't eat meat, as it's a great source of protein. *Paneer* has the consistency of solid ricotta cheese. *Paneer* can be found in many grocery stores these days, but it's also pretty easy to make. (See page 98.) If you want to avoid milk-based products, substitute cubed, firm tofu. It's lighter, but other than that it's hard to tell the difference.

Rice (*chawal*): Basmati is among the most coveted varieties of rice in the world. The word itself means fragrance in Sanskrit, which is appropriate. The kernels are long, slender, and almost perfumed. I can still smell the exact combination of rice and whole spices cooking in my childhood home before any big party. True basmati is only grown in North India, around the city of Dehra Dun. These days, as people become more health conscious, there has been a move to eat the rice in its more original form, brown basmati, and other brown rice varieties.

Tomatoes: With Indian food, the key is to include just the right amount of tart to offset the spice. So, when you purchase tomatoes, forgo the overly ripe and overly sweet ones, or

save them for your salad. I like to use plum tomatoes, which are the right size and taste for Indian cooking.

Yogurt (*dai/dhai*): Unlike in the West, in India we eat savory or salty yogurt with meals and save the sweetened for dessert. We also make our own yogurt, which makes for a slightly thinner, more sour variety than that found in most grocery stores. Use whatever plain yogurt is available, but try to make it one day and you might realize how easy and rewarding the process is.

Legumes: Lentils, Beans, & Peas

LEGUMES ARE SIMPLY SEEDS THAT GROW WITHIN PODS. THEY COME IN many shapes and sizes and are a huge part of the Indian diet, acting as a high-protein, low-fat option for hundreds of thousands of vegetarians. Legumes are also high in fiber, folate, potassium, iron, magnesium, and phytochemicals—a group of compounds that may help prevent degenerative diseases such as cardiovascular disease and cancer.

Legumes include lentils, beans, and peas. I like to purchase mine dried rather than in cans because dried are not only cheaper, they also break down better during the cooking process. Canned beans and lentils are already saturated with liquid, so they won't absorb any cooking liquid and thus won't break down as well. This book will teach you how to cook dried legumes in just a few simple steps in a slow cooker.

The variety of available beans and lentils, let alone the prospect of learning how to effectively cook each one, can be overwhelming. Some are better known by their English name and some by their Hindi counterpart, so I've tried to make identification as simple as possible. Each legume is listed by its English name first, followed by all the alternatives. Keep in mind that most lentils can be purchased in four different forms:

1. The original, whole lentil with the skin intact. Usually the word *sabut or sabud,* which means "whole" in Hindi, precedes the name of the lentil to indicate that it is in its original form, with nothing removed. This is obviously the healthiest form of any lentil, but it takes longer to cook because the skin is thicker and the lentil has not been cut.

2. The whole lentil without skin.

3. The split lentil with the skin on (called *chilkha,* which means "skin" in Hindi).

4. The split lentil with no skin (called *duhli,* which means "washed" in Hindi).

Amazingly, the different forms of one type of lentil—though they all start from the same source—can have strikingly different results when used in the same recipe. Cooking times will vary. Generally, anything with the skin on will take longer to cook but will also be more nutritious than its skinned and split counterpart.

Many of these legumes are also referred to by the generic term *dal.* I grew up in a Punjabi household, where *dals* referred to soupy lentils. But folks from other parts of India call soupy beans, dry lentils, dry beans, and even lentils cooked with rice *dals.* Don't let the term throw you off.

That said, a wonderful variety of legumes are now available in mainstream grocery stores, although they will be less expensive if you can find them at an Indian grocery store. Most members of the Indian community have a favorite Indian grocer they'll visit once a month or so to stock up on the basics. If you are going to make a habit of eating legumes, it makes sense to buy them in larger, cheaper quantities. I buy dried lentils in 4-pound bags. Buying online is another great option.

Important! Regardless of where you purchase the legumes, it's a good idea to quickly sift through them before you use them or transfer them to another container. Often, bits of debris, small rocks, and other particles get mixed in with the product, and you'd never want a guest to chomp down on a piece of gravel. Never wash dried legumes until you're ready to cook, as storing them with any moisture can spoil the whole batch.

To sift through the lentils and beans, simply take a white plate (one with a pattern will distract the eye) and pour about a cup of the lentils on the side furthest away from you. Quickly bring small amounts of the lentils towards you with your hand. If you see any foreign particles and rocks simply pick them out and throw them away. Once I've sorted through them, I store the legumes into labeled plastic containers I keep lined up on my pantry shelf. Some of my friends prefer glass containers. Either way, labeled containers provide easier access when cooking.

When you are ready to cook them, put the dried legumes in a deep bowl or right in your slow cooker. Cover them with water and scrub them clean with your hands. The water will look murky the first couple of times; just throw it away and repeat the process a few times with clean water.

At times you'll get a bad batch of legumes. If you find a powder at the bottom of the bag or tiny holes through the legumes, the batch may have been infested by insects. If this is the case, throw away the entire batch and start over.

Most legumes, once cooked, will keep for about three days in the refrigerator and for up to three months in the freezer. You can reheat them in the microwave or on the stovetop. I prefer the stove because it enables me to reconstitute the dish a bit, and I personally believe it's safer. Usually, as they sit, legumes continue to absorb more water. So, don't be surprised when you pull a dish out of the refrigerator and find that it's thicker than when you put it in. All you have to do is add a little water and heat it slowly. Remember, you'll have to compensate for the diluted flavor by adding a bit more salt and maybe some red chile pepper.

The variety of beans and lentils out there is almost mind blowing. I only list those that are most commonly used in Indian cooking. If you see another legume that looks interesting, bring it home and try it in one of the recipes listed in this book. You may just create your own favorite dish.

Black lentils, black gram (*urad, maa, matpe beans*): This lentil is one of the best-known throughout India, especially because of its use in many Hindu ceremonies. It's easy to recognize because it's jet black, tiny, and oval-shaped. Like other lentils it comes in four forms: whole with the skin on (*sabut urad*), whole with the skin off, split with the skin on (*urad dal*), and split with the skin off. Of course, the first form is the most nutritious. The other forms of this lentil have their own unique textures and qualities when cooked. Removing the skin and splitting the lentil makes it creamier and easier to digest.

Brown lentils (*masoor, masar, mussoor*): These dark, round lentils are usually sold and used skinned and split. In this form, they are almost salmon in color and better known in the West as "red lentils" or *masoor dal*. A bit bizarre, but when cooked they turn yellow. They cook quickly and make a very easy meal when you're short on time.

Cowpeas, black-eyed peas/beans (*lobhia, rongi*), and red cowpeas (*sabut chowli*): When you think of black-eyed peas, cooking from the Southern region of the United States usually comes to mind: simple comfort food. It makes sense, as these beans originated in Africa. Black-eyed peas are white or beige in color with a black spot in the middle. Red cowpeas are reddish brown in color, with an oval shape and a black spot in the middle. Both varieties make a great Indian curry, with their earthy, filling taste, and are especially good when mixed with greens or coconut milk.

Chickpeas (*chana*): Who would have thought that chickpeas could be so varied and interesting? Most of us are used to the chickpea that is used most commonly around the world: the yellow chickpea, chickpea, or Bengal gram. In Hindi, it's called *kabuli chana*, and it's used in dishes that have a lot of gravy and dishes where the beans are cooked until soft, but with little gravy.

A lesser-known variety of the traditional chickpea is the black chickpea, or *kala chana*. As its name suggests, this bean looks like a chickpea, but it's about half the size and blackish brown. It's extremely high in protein and needs to be cooked longer than its white counterpart. Even after cooking, though, keep in mind that this bean is a tough little cookie. It will never be as soft or break down as much as other beans and lentils. But don't worry—it's still delicious.

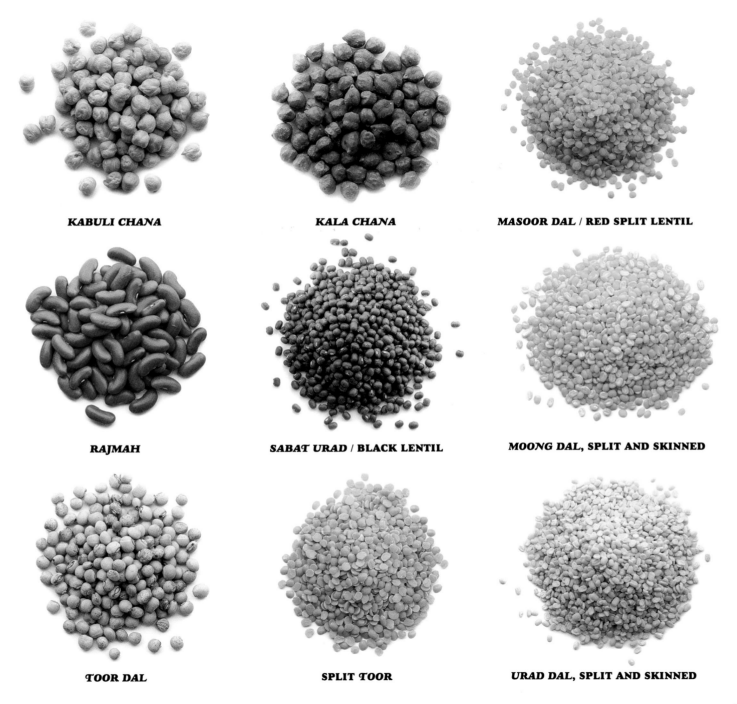

KABULI CHANA

KALA CHANA

MASOOR DAL / RED SPLIT LENTIL

RAJMAH

SABAT URAD / BLACK LENTIL

MOONG DAL, SPLIT AND SKINNED

TOOR DAL

SPLIT TOOR

URAD DAL, SPLIT AND SKINNED

At most Indian grocery stores, you will also see green chickpeas, or *hara chana*. These are just like black chickpea in size and shape, but they're green in color. When cooked, the green chickpea doesn't look or taste much different from the black chickpea.

Split gram (*chana dal*): This is probably one of the most common lentils in India. It's derived from skinning and splitting the black chickpea. It makes a delicious, hearty stew. When raw, it looks a lot like the split and skinned version of *toor dal*, so be sure to label your containers.

Green lentils, green gram (*moong, mung*): These lentils look like their black counterparts in size and shape, but they are green in color. They also cook faster than black lentils. This lentil comes in three forms: whole with the skin (*sabut moong*), split with the skin (*mung dal*), and split without the skin (*yellow mung*). This last form is one of the fastest-cooking and best-known *dals* in North India. It's easy on the stomach, so it is often made without spices to soothe a stomachache.

Kidney beans (*rajmah*): As its name suggests, this is a kidney-shaped bean that is red in color. Many types of kidney beans are available: dark red, light red, and *Jammu* and *Kashmiri rajmah*. Some prefer the *Kashmiri rajmah* because it's smaller and more delicate than the other varieties, but I prefer the light red because it breaks down better in the cooking process. Every household in North India has its own way of cooking this bean, which shows you how important it is to this region of India.

Pigeon peas: This category encompasses all of the forms of *toor dal* (*toovar, arhar*, and *tur*). This lentil is used quite a bit in South and West India. When whole (*sabut toor*), the lentil is small, round, and tan in color. This form is used primarily in West India. When split and skinned (*toor dal*), it has a yellowish-beige color and is the primary base for *sambhar*, a spicy soup eaten in South India with savory crepes called *dosas*. It can be purchased dry or oily. The oily version is covered with vegetable oil to increase the shelf life of the lentils and to prevent contamination from insects. If you buy the oily variety, be sure to wash them thoroughly before using to get rid of that top layer of oil.

Yellow split peas: These are the dried yellow version of the green pea. They are wonderful when cooked in a slow cooker and blended into a soup.

Indians Love Their Bread

BREAD IS JUST AS IMPORTANT AS RICE TO MANY INDIANS, ESPECIALLY in the northern region of Punjab where golden wheat fields are a natural and beautiful part of the landscape. My father was raised in Bhikhi, a tiny village in the heart of this state. His father was a landowner who managed many of the wheat and mustard green fields that dominated the harvest. There, some form of bread is served with every meal, and rice is served only on special occasions.

Naan: Most non-Indians know *naan*, which has become synonymous with Indian bread. The irony here is that Indians themselves really only eat *naan* on special occasions, and we rarely make it at home. *Naan* is a leavened bread made from white flour and is traditionally cooked on the walls of a *tandoor*, or clay oven. When we eat out, my mother prefers to order *tandoori roti*, which is cooked in the same manner as *naan* but made with healthier whole-wheat flour.

Parantha: Usually eaten for breakfast, this unleavened flat bread is essentially a stuffed *roti*. You take the same dough for *rotis* and stuff a ball of it with anything from spiced potatoes to cauliflower, or even just chopped onions and chiles. *Paranthas* are usually thicker and heavier than *rotis*. Both are cooked on a heavy cast-iron griddle known as a *tava*. Toward the end of cooking, a teaspoon of oil or *ghee* is usually spread across the *parantha* to give it a golden sheen.

Poori: Talk about the ultimate comfort food. *Pooris* hit the mark! The dough is a little harder than that used to make *rotis*. Once the ball of dough is rolled out thin, it is put in a deep wok-like pan, called a *karahi*, that is filled with hot oil. The flat dough will initially sink to the bottom, but as it cooks it will rise to the top of the oil in seconds and puff up.

Roti, Chapati, Phulka: The healthiest and most common bread in India is *roti*, unleavened flat bread that is rolled out thin by hand and heated until golden brown. Traditionally, *rotis* are made from 100 percent whole-wheat flour. Outside of India, the best way to make them is to purchase *chapati* or *aata* flour from an Indian grocery store. The type of wheat used for *chapati* flour is made from durum wheat rather than hard red. It is softer and produces fluffier *rotis* than other kinds of flour.

When buying *chapati* flour, be careful that it's not a mix of whole-wheat and white flours. The purest, made of all whole-wheat flour, will be the healthiest choice.

How to Eat Indian Food

THERE'S A LOCAL WAY TO EAT ANY CUISINE. INDIAN FOOD IS NO EXCEPTION. In traditional North Indian households there are predominantly seven elements to any formal meal:

1. A wet curry made of veggies, legumes, or meat

2. A dry veggie dish (*sabzi*) like cauliflower and potatoes or pan-fried okra

3. Bread like *naan*, *roti*, or *poori* and/or rice

4. A side salad of sliced raw onions, cucumbers, and tomatoes with lemon juice, white salt, black salt, and a little red chile pepper

5. *Aachar*, which is a dollop of spicy pickle made from chile peppers, lemon, or mango, or a chutney made of mint or tamarind

6. Yogurt eaten plain or savory, as *raita*, with chopped veggies and spices

7. *Papard*, a crispy, spicy blend of lentils ground wafer thin. It becomes crispy after it's heated on the stovetop

Normally, we put rice or bread on a large dinner plate along with a scoop of the dry *sabzi*. The wet curry goes in a small bowl to the side. In another bowl is the yogurt. We take a few pieces of salad and put it on our large plate along with a piece of *papard* and *aachar* or *chutney*.

To eat, break off a piece of the bread and make a scoop out of it. Dip one end lightly into the *aachar* or *chutney*, and scoop up some dry *sabzi* and then some wet curry. Once that's in your mouth, it's followed by a piece of salad—usually a piece of onion. If eating rice instead of bread, use your spoon or fork to mix the above dishes in the same order and again chase once in your mouth with some salad. Pieces of *papard* are eaten in between for crunch and spoonfuls of yogurt cool everything down. Yes, there are many tastes and textures here, but that's the point. It's like an explosion of flavors in your mouth with every bite.

These days, with the hectic schedules of parents and kids alike, it's next to impossible to sit down to such intricate meals every night. So, in my house we usually sit down with bread or rice, a dry or wet dish, salad, and yogurt. All the rest is a bonus.

Lentils

"Amazingly, the different forms of one type of lentil—though they all start from the same source—can have strikingly different results when used in the same recipe."

Simplest of Simple Yellow Lentils

Black Lentils

Kaali dal, sabut urad, whole black gram, maa, whole matpe beans | SLOW COOKER SIZE: **5-QUART** • COOKING TIME: **8 HOURS ON HIGH** • YIELD: **14 CUPS (3.31 L)**

This is a staple dish in North India, where it is known as the queen of all *dals*. It is also referred to as *maa di dal*. Translated literally this means "Mother's lentils," which pretty much says it all in terms of how Punjabis view this dish. When cooked over a slow fire, the dish is incredibly rich and hearty. Most North Indian restaurants turn it into *dal makhani* by adding butter or cream.

Because this is a tougher lentil than most, it usually takes longer to cook on the stovetop. It's often cooked over the lowest of flames in a heavy pot overnight, which is why it's so helpful to have a slow cooker to do all the legwork for you. Cooking this dish slowly and for a longer period of time breaks the lentils down to a point where you may not even need to add cream and butter. I never do. But, if you prefer it richer, by all means add it in! The mustard oil is optional, but my *nani* (maternal grandmother) always added it to help the lentils break open and infuse them with flavor.

3 cups (603g) whole, dried black lentils with skin, cleaned and washed thoroughly

1 medium yellow or red onion, peeled and quartered

1 (2-inch [5 cm]) piece ginger, peeled and roughly chopped

4 cloves garlic, peeled

4 –6 Thai, serrano, or cayenne chiles, stems removed

2 bunches fresh cilantro, washed and chopped (about 2 cups [473 mL]), divided

1 tablespoon (15 mL) ground cumin

1 tablespoon (15 mL) ground coriander

1 tablespoon (15 mL) garam masala

1 heaping tablespoon (20 mL) sea salt

1 teaspoon (5 mL) turmeric powder

1 teaspoon–1 tablespoon (5–15 mL) red chile powder

12 cups (2.84 L) water

1 teaspoon (5 mL) mustard oil (optional)

½ cup (118 mL) heavy whipping cream or plain yogurt (optional)

1 pat butter for garnish (optional)

Chopped onions, for garnish

Chopped tomatoes, for garnish

1. Put the black lentils in the slow cooker.

2. In a food processor, grind the onion, ginger, garlic, green chiles, and 1 cup (201 g) of the cilantro. Add this mixture to the lentils along with the cumin, coriander, *garam masala*, sea salt, turmeric, red chile powder, and water.

3. Cook on high for 4 hours. Add the mustard oil, if desired.

4. Cook for another 4 hours. Mix in the remaining cilantro and add the cream or yogurt, if you wish. Garnish with a pat of butter and chopped onions and tomatoes. Serve with basmati or brown rice or with *roti* or *naan*, an onion salad, and yogurt.

To make this dish in a 3½-quart slow cooker, halve all the ingredients and proceed with the recipe. A half recipe makes 8 cups (1.89 L).

Black Lentils with Kidney Beans

Sabut Kaali Dal aur Rajmah | SLOW COOKER SIZE: **5-QUART** • COOKING TIME: **8 HOURS ON HIGH** • YIELD: **14 CUPS (3.31 L)**

Whole black lentil and kidney bean curry was a staple in my husband's childhood home. My mother-in-law makes the best I've ever tasted. It's a nice variation from the traditional black lentil recipe. Slicing the ginger into thin strips is worth the extra effort for the heightened flavor and unique texture it provides.

2 cups (402 g) whole, dried black lentils with skin, cleaned and washed thoroughly

1 cup (201 g) dried red kidney beans, cleaned and washed thoroughly

1 medium yellow or red onion, peeled and quartered

4 cloves garlic, peeled

4–6 green Thai, serrano, or cayenne chiles, stems removed

1 (2-inch [5 cm]) piece ginger, peeled and sliced into 1-inch (2.5 cm) matchsticks

1 tablespoon (15 mL) ground cumin

1 tablespoon (15 mL) ground coriander

1 tablespoon (15 mL) garam masala

1 heaping tablespoon (20 mL) sea salt

1 teaspoon (5 mL) turmeric powder

1 teaspoon–1 tablespoon (5–15 mL) red chile powder

12 cups (2.84 L) water

2 tablespoons (30 mL) chopped fresh cilantro

1. Put the lentils and kidney beans in the slow cooker.

2. In a food processor, puree the onion, garlic, and green chiles. Add this mixture to the slow cooker along with the ginger.

3. Add the cumin, coriander, *garam masala*, sea salt, turmeric, red chile powder, and water to the slow cooker.

4. Cook on high for 8 hours.

5. Stir in the cilantro. Serve with basmati or brown rice or *roti* or *naan*, a side of onion salad, and *raita*.

To make this dish in a 3½-quart slow cooker, halve all the ingredients and proceed with the recipe. A half recipe makes 8 cups (1.89 L).

Black Lentils with Kidney Beans and Chickpeas

Teen Taal dal, Three Note Dal | SLOW COOKER SIZE: **5-QUART** • COOKING TIME: **7 HOURS ON HIGH** • YIELD: **11 CUPS (2.60 L)**

This dish is a meal in itself. The mix of kidney beans and chickpeas gives it an almost meaty texture. I adapted this recipe from Raghavan Iyer's *660 Curries* and modified it for the slow cooker. It's fancy enough to serve to guests but easy enough to make for your family as well.

1 cup (201 g) whole, dried black lentils with skin, cleaned and washed thoroughly

1 cup (201 g) dried chickpeas, cleaned and washed thoroughly

1 cup (201 g) dried kidney beans, cleaned and washed thoroughly

3 fresh or dried Indian bay leaves

3 pods green cardamom

1 (4-inch [10 cm]) cinnamon stick

1 small yellow or red onion, peeled

1 (2-inch [5 cm]) piece of ginger, peeled

4 cloves garlic, peeled

4–6 green Thai, serrano, or cayenne chiles, stems removed

1 tablespoon (15 mL) cumin seeds

1 tablespoon (15 mL) coriander seeds

2 tablespoons (30 mL) canola or vegetable oil

1 teaspoon (5 mL) turmeric powder

1 teaspoon–1 tablespoon (5–15 mL) red chile powder

2 tablespoons (30 mL) sea salt

2 tablespoons (30 mL) tomato paste

½ cup (118 mL) plain yogurt

9 cups (2.13 L) water

¼ cup (59 mL) heavy whipping cream

2 tablespoons (30 mL) chopped fresh cilantro

1. Put the lentils, chickpeas, kidney beans, bay leaves, cardamom, and cinnamon in the slow cooker.

2. In a food processor, grind the onion, ginger, garlic, and green chiles into a paste. The paste will be a bit watery from the onion.

3. In a dry frying pan over medium-high heat, roast the cumin and coriander seeds. This will take 2 to 3 minutes. You'll need to stand there, shake the pan a few times, and wait for the seeds to brown. Don't overcook them, or they'll burn. Put the roasted seeds in a dish to cool. Once they're cool (about 15 minutes), grind them in a coffee grinder reserved for spices or with a mortar and pestle.

4. Heat the oil over medium-high in a shallow frying pan. Add the onion mixture and sauté for 5 to 7 minutes, until browned. Add the ground cumin-coriander blend, turmeric, red chile powder, and sea salt, and continue to cook for about 4 minutes, scraping the bottom of the pan to prevent scorching. Add the mixture to the slow cooker. If any of it sticks to the frying pan, add a little water and scrape it out into the slow cooker.

5. Add the tomato paste and water to the slow cooker.

6. Cook on high for 6½ hours.

7. Add the yogurt and cream. Replace the lid and simmer for another 30 minutes.

8. Remove the whole spices and top with the cilantro. Serve with basmati or brown rice or thick *roti* or *naan*.

Try This! Think of this as a thick chili. Break a few tortilla chips on top, add some grated cheddar cheese, and serve to your kids as a one-bowl meal. They'll eat it up. It would also make a great dish for a Super Bowl party.

To make this dish in a 3½-quart slow cooker, halve all the ingredients and proceed with the recipe. A half recipe makes 6 cups (1.42 L).

Split Black Lentils

Urad dal Chilkha | SLOW COOKER SIZE: **5-QUART** • COOKING TIME: **6 HOURS ON HIGH** • YIELD: **17 CUPS (4.022 L)**

This is one of my favorite *dals* because it's so easy to make and comes out incredibly rich and creamy. The creaminess comes from the way the lentils break down after cooking rather than actual cream. Using lentils with the skin intact makes this dish more nutritious. Don't overcook this one, as it tends to get a little bitter.

3 cups (603 g) dried split black lentils with skin, cleaned and washed thoroughly

1 small yellow or red onion, peeled and finely chopped

1 small tomato, finely chopped

1 (1-inch [2.5 cm]) piece ginger, peeled and sliced in 1-inch (2.5 cm) long strips

2 cloves garlic, peeled and finely chopped

4–6 green Thai, serrano or cayenne chiles, stems removed

1 tablespoon (15 mL) cumin seeds

1 heaping tablespoon (20 mL) sea salt

1 teaspoon (5 mL) turmeric powder

1 teaspoon–1 tablespoon (5–15 mL) red chile powder

12 cups (2.84 L) water

2 tablespoons (30 mL) chopped fresh cilantro

1. Put the lentils, onion, tomato, ginger, garlic, green chiles, cumin, sea salt, turmeric, red chile powder, and water in the slow cooker.

2. Cook on high for 6 hours.

3. Garnish with cilantro and serve with basmati or brown rice, an onion salad, and a yogurt *raita* on the side.

Try This! Substitute split green lentils with skin for the split black lentils for a slightly different taste.

To make this dish in a 3½-quart slow cooker, halve all the ingredients and proceed with the recipe. A half recipe makes 7 cups (1.66 L).

Simplest of Simple Yellow Lentils

Dhuli Moong Dal | SLOW COOKER SIZE: **5-QUART** • COOKING TIME: **7 HOURS ON LOW** • YIELD: **14 CUPS (3.31 L)**

Every Monday, my father-in-law eats yellow *moong dal* for dinner. It's a staple for many Indians because it cooks quickly and is easy to digest. When I worked, I made this for my kids almost every night—often because I was too tired to try anything else. I'd come home, fill a shot glass with the lentils and some brown rice, add water, and play with the kids until it cooked. It actually made enough for both their dinners! The slow cooker just means I don't have to worry about it overflowing or burning.

3 cups (603 g) dried, split, and skinned yellow moong dal, cleaned and washed thoroughly

1 medium yellow or red onion, peeled and finely chopped

1 medium tomato, finely chopped

1 (1-inch [2.5 cm]) piece ginger, peeled and grated or finely chopped

2–3 cloves garlic, peeled and minced, grated, or finely chopped

2–4 Thai, serrano, or cayenne chiles, stems removed, finely chopped

1 tablespoon (15 mL) cumin seeds

1 heaping tablespoon (20 mL) sea salt

2 teaspoons (10 mL) turmeric powder

1 teaspoon–1 tablespoon (5–15 mL) red chile powder

12 cups (2.84 L) water

1 tablespoon (15 mL) chopped cilantro

1. Put the lentils, onion, tomato, ginger, garlic, green chiles, cumin, sea salt, turmeric, red chile powder, and water in the slow cooker.

2. Cook on low for 7 hours, until the lentils break down.

3. Garnish with cilantro. Top with a dollop of butter and chopped onions and serve over a bowl of steaming, fragrant basmati or brown rice or with *roti* or *naan*.

Try This! Chop up about 2 cups of fresh Swiss chard and add it at the very end. Replace the lid and let the chard sit in the slow cooker for a few minutes before serving.

To make this dish in a 3½-quart slow cooker, halve all the ingredients and proceed with the recipe. A half recipe makes 8 cups (1.89 L).

Simple Spinach and Lentil Soup

Palak aur Dhuli Moong Dal | SLOW COOKER SIZE: **5-QUART** • COOKING TIME: **6 HOURS ON LOW** • YIELD: **14 CUPS (3.31 L)**

I always knew yellow lentils and spinach went well together, but I was inspired to try the combination again after seeing a recipe in Anjum Anand's *Indian Food Made Easy*. I've modified it for the slow cooker, and I'm so glad I did. Cook just until the lentils break open—you don't want them to break down too much. And add the spinach at the very end to keep it bright green and fresh. This is one of the few recipes I prefer without any onions or chiles. I ate this by the spoonful right out of my slow cooker the first time I whipped it up.

3 cups (603 g) dried, split, and skinned yellow moong dal, cleaned and washed thoroughly

1 (1-inch [2.5 cm]) piece ginger, peeled and grated or ground in a food processor

2 cloves garlic, peeled and minced, grated, or ground in a food processor

1 teaspoon (5 mL) tomato paste

1 teaspoon (5 mL) cumin seeds

1 teaspoon (5 mL) ground coriander

1 teaspoon (5 mL) garam masala

1 teaspoon (5 mL) turmeric powder

2 tablespoons (30 mL) sea salt

12 cups (2.84 L) water

4 cups (804 g) firmly packed spinach leaves, washed and coarsely chopped

1. Put the lentils, ginger, garlic, tomato paste, cumin, coriander, *garam masala*, turmeric, sea salt, and water in the slow cooker.

2. Cook on low for 6 hours, then add the spinach. Turn off the slow cooker and let sit for 15 minutes with the lid on. Serve as a soup or over basmati or brown rice.

To make this dish in a 3½-quart slow cooker, halve all the ingredients and proceed with the recipe. A half recipe makes 8 cups (1.89 L).

Green Spinach Lentils

Palak aur Sabut Moong Dal | SLOW COOKER SIZE: **5-QUART** • COOKING TIME: **7 HOURS ON HIGH** • YIELD: **14 CUPS (3.31 L)**

My Nisha auntie in Chandigarh, India gave me the recipe for this *dal*. Talk about packed with nutrition! It mixes the whole, green *moong* lentil with iron-rich spinach to create a dish you'll love making again and again!

3 cups (603 g) whole dried green lentils with skin, cleaned and washed thoroughly

1 medium yellow or red onion, peeled and finely chopped

1 medium tomato, diced

1 (1-inch [2.5 cm]) piece ginger, peeled and chopped or grated

2–3 cloves garlic, peeled and chopped or grated

3–4 green Thai, serrano, or cayenne chiles, stems removed, finely chopped

1 tablespoon (15 mL) cumin seeds

2 tablespoons (30 mL) sea salt

½ teaspoon (2.5 mL) garam masala

1 teaspoon (5 mL) turmeric powder

1 teaspoon (5 mL) red chile powder

12 cups (2.84 L) water

4 cups (804 g) firmly packed spinach leaves, washed and chopped

1. Put the lentils, onion, tomato, ginger, garlic, green chiles, cumin, sea salt, *garam masala*, turmeric, red chile powder, and water in the slow cooker.

2. Cook on high for 6½ hours. Add the spinach and cook for 30 more minutes.

3. Serve over steaming basmati or brown rice or eat with *roti* or *naan*.

Try This! Make this dish without the spinach—the more traditional way to eat it.

To make this dish in a 3½-quart slow cooker, halve all the ingredients and proceed with the recipe. A half recipe makes 8 cups (1.89 L).

Tart Whole Pigeon Peas

Khata Sabut Toor Dal | SLOW COOKER SIZE: **5-QUART** • COOKING TIME: **4 HOURS ON HIGH** • YIELD: **10 CUPS (2.37 L)**

I didn't grow up eating whole *toor dal*. In fact, my mother can't recall a time she's eaten this lentil in its whole form, either. It's more common in Western India. My experimentation, however, paid off with a fast, easy recipe that produces a wonderful, almost meaty accompaniment to a salad.

3 cups (603 g) dried, whole toor dal with skin, cleaned and washed thoroughly

9 cups (2.13 L) water

2 tablespoons (30 mL) vegetable or canola oil

1 tablespoon (15 mL) black mustard seeds

10–15 fresh curry leaves

1 large yellow or red onion, peeled and coarsely chopped

1 (1-inch [2.5 cm]) piece ginger, peeled and grated

4 cloves garlic, peeled and minced or grated

4–6 whole green Thai, serrano, or cayenne chiles, stems removed, halved lengthwise

5–6 dried red chiles

1 teaspoon (5 mL) ground coriander

1 heaping tablespoon (20 mL) sea salt

Juice of 1 lemon

1. Put the lentils and water in the slow cooker. Cook on high for 3 hours. After cooking, if there is too much water left, drain and discard the excess water. This should be a dry dish that can pass for a side salad.

2. Heat the oil in a frying pan over medium-high heat. Once it's hot, add the mustard seeds. Cover the pan until the seeds pop (this takes just a few minutes—make sure they don't burn). Add the curry leaves, onion, ginger, garlic, green chiles, red chiles, and coriander. Cook, stirring several times, until the onions are browned.

3. Add this mixture to the slow cooker along with the sea salt. Cook for another hour. Sprinkle with lemon juice. Enjoy with hot *roti* or *naan* or as a side salad.

To make this dish in a 3½-quart slow cooker, halve all the ingredients and proceed with the recipe. A half recipe makes 5 cups (1.18 L).

South Indian Lentils with Curry Leaves

Parippu Curry | SLOW COOKER SIZE: **5-QUART** • COOKING TIME: **6 HOURS ON LOW** • YIELD: **11 CUPS (2.60 L)**

In North India, lentils are called *dals*, while in South India they are called *parippu*. While *parippu* can be made with various types of lentils, this recipe uses red split *masoor* lentils and holds to tradition by including curry leaves and coconut milk. I've adapted it for the slow cooker from one of my favorite Indian cookbooks, *A Little Taste of…India*.

Even though I didn't grow up eating lentils cooked this way, it's now hands down one of my favorite lentil preparations. I could eat fresh curry leaves every day. *Masoor dal* starts red but cooks to a yellow color.

3 cups (603 g) dried, split, and skinned masoor dal, *cleaned and washed thoroughly*

1 medium yellow or red onion, peeled and coarsely chopped

2 medium tomatoes, finely chopped

2–4 green Thai, serrano, or cayenne chiles, stems removed, finely chopped

1 teaspoon (5 mL) ground cumin

1 teaspoon (5 mL) ground coriander

½ teaspoon (2.5 mL) turmeric powder

2 tablespoons (30 mL) sea salt

9 cups (2.13 L) water

2 tablespoons (30 mL) vegetable or canola oil

2 teaspoons (10 mL) cumin seeds

1 teaspoon (5 mL) black or yellow mustard seeds

½ medium yellow or red onion, peeled and finely chopped

15–20 fresh curry leaves

1 (14-oz. [414 mL]) can coconut milk

1. Put the lentils, coarsely chopped onion, tomatoes, green chiles, cumin, coriander, turmeric, sea salt, and water in the slow cooker.

2. Cook on low for 5½ hours.

3. Heat the oil over medium-high in a frying pan. Once hot, add cumin and mustard seeds. Cover and cook until the mustard seeds pop. Add the finely chopped onion and the curry leaves and fry, stirring constantly, until lightly browned. Be careful, as the leaves are delicate and can burn easily. Add to the slow cooker along with the coconut milk.

4. Stir and cook for another 30 minutes.

5. Serve over basmati or brown rice.

To make this dish in a 3½-quart slow cooker, halve all the ingredients and proceed with the recipe. A half recipe makes 6 cups (1.42 L).

South Indian Pigeon Peas and Vegetable Stew

Sambhar | SLOW COOKER SIZE: **5-QUART** • COOKING TIME: **11 HOURS ON HIGH** • YIELD: **17 CUPS (4 L)**

This is one of the most popular South Indian lentil stews. Traditionally, it is eaten for breakfast or lunch with steamed *idlis* or large paper-thin savory crepes called *dosas*. My friends and family are still amazed that I can make this dish taste so authentic coming from a slow cooker, but I've done it many times over.

You can make this with store-bought *sambhar masala*, but I guarantee if you make the *masala* mix yourself you will never go back.

2 cups (402 g) dried toor dal, skinned and split, cleaned and washed thoroughly

1 large yellow or red onion, peeled and coarsely chopped

1 medium tomato, coarsely chopped

2–3 carrots, peeled and chopped

1 medium russet, Yukon Gold, or red potato, peeled and chopped

1 medium daikon, peeled and cut into 2½–inch (6 cm) strips

1 small turnip, peeled and chopped

5–6 dried red chiles

11 cups (2.6 L) water

2 heaping tablespoons (50 mL) tamarind paste

3–4 heaping tablespoons (75–100 mL) sambhar masala (recipe follows)

3 tablespoons (45 mL) sea salt

2 tablespoons (30 mL) vegetable or canola oil

1 tablespoon (15 mL) black mustard seeds

10–15 fresh curry leaves

1. Put the *toor dal*, onion, tomato, carrots, potato, daikon, turnip, dried red chiles and water in the slow cooker. Cook on high for 10 hours. At this point, the *dal* will start to break down.

2. Add the tamarind paste, *sambhar masala*, and sea salt to the slow cooker and cook for another hour. (Tamarind paste is sticky and difficult to get off the measuring spoon. I take the paste on the spoon and dip it into the hot liquid to clean the spoon off. Just be sure to wash and dry the spoon before dipping it back into the tamarind paste and repeating.)

3. You can substitute other vegetables as long as they add up to about 8 cups. I've used string beans, okra, eggplant, cauliflower, parsnips, and small pearl onions. South Indians also use a long, green vegetable called a drumstick, which is rarely found fresh in the United States but can be found in cans at well-stocked Indian grocers.

(continued on page 62)

(continued from page 61)

4. At the very end of cooking, heat the oil in a small frying pan over medium-high heat. Once it begins to smoke slightly, add the mustard seeds, cover, and cook until they pop. Add the curry leaves and cook 1–2 minutes, stirring constantly to prevent burning, until slightly browned. Add this mixture to the slow cooker very carefully, as the hot oil may splash once it hits the liquid.

5. Serve with *idli*, *dosa*, or rice. My kids often enjoy this dish as a nourishing soup.

To make this dish in a 3½-quart slow cooker, halve all the ingredients and proceed with the recipe. A half recipe makes 8–10 cups (1.89–2.37 L).

Note: The absolute best *sambhars* are made with homemade *masala*. I put off trying to make it most of my life, thinking there was a secret to it that was beyond my grasp. It's actually not hard at all! Make a batch and store it in an airtight container for up to 2 months.

Sambhar Masala

I have loved this recipe from Raghavan Iyer's *600 Curries* from the moment I tried it.

½ cup (100 g) firmly packed medium-large fresh curry leaves

½ cup (100 g) dried red Thai or cayenne chiles

¼ cup (50 g) chana dal

¼ cup (50 g) coriander seeds

2 tablespoons (30 mL) cumin seeds

1 tablespoon (15 mL) fenugreek seeds

1 tablespoon (15 mL) black or yellow mustard seeds

1 tablespoon (15 mL) white poppy seeds

2 (4-inch [10 cm]) cinnamon sticks, broken into pieces

1 tablespoon (15 mL) unrefined sesame oil or canola oil

1. Combine all the spices in a bowl. Drizzle the oil over them and mix well.

2. Heat a skillet over medium-high heat. Add the *chana dal* and the spice mixture and cook, stirring constantly, until the curry leaves brown and curl up and the other spices brown, about 3 to 4 minutes.

3. Immediately transfer the mixture to a plate and allow to cool for about 20 minutes. Once the mixture is cool, grind it in a coffee grinder reserved for spices. Store it in an air-tight container for up to 2 months.

Try This! Enjoy this *masala* sprinkled on popcorn for an Indian twist to family movie nights.

Garlic and Chile Split Pigeon Pea Curry

Lasan aur Lal Mirch Toor Dal | SLOW COOKER SIZE: **5-QUART** • COOKING TIME: **6 HOURS ON HIGH** • YIELD: **16 CUPS (3.79 L)**

Anjum Anand's *Indian Food Made Easy* inspired me to try this dish, and I'm so glad I did. It expanded my repertoire of lentil curries and helped me find another *dal* that my girls actually enjoy eating. The lemon adds a great flavor and a tartness that most Indians enjoy in their foods.

Don't let the dried chiles deceive you. They're included more for looks and subtle flavor rather than for heat, which is balanced by the lemon. Even my four-year-old was able to eat this dish.

3 cups (603 g) dried toor dal, skinned and split, cleaned and washed thoroughly

1 (2-inch [5 cm]) piece ginger, peeled and grated

4–6 cloves garlic, peeled and grated or minced

10 dried red chiles

1 teaspoon (5 mL) turmeric powder

2 tablespoons (30 mL) sea salt

11 cups (2.60 L) water

2 tablespoons (30 mL) fresh lemon juice

1. Put the lentils, ginger, garlic, dried chiles, turmeric, sea salt, and water in the slow cooker. Cook on high for 6 hours.

2. Add the lemon juice just before serving. Enjoy with basmati or brown rice or with *roti* or *naan*, an onion salad, and yogurt *raita*.

To make this dish in a 3½-quart slow cooker, halve all the ingredients and proceed with the recipe. A half recipe makes 8 cups (1.89 L).

Simple Split Chickpea Curry

Chana Dal | SLOW COOKER SIZE: **5-QUART** • COOKING TIME: **8 HOURS ON HIGH** • YIELD: **10 CUPS (2.37 L)**

Both of my kids love this dish. There's something about the consistency of the lentils that makes them hearty but light at the same time. This is a good alternative to *toor dal*, which has a muskier taste and smell.

3 cups (603 g) dried chana dal, split and skinned, cleaned and washed thoroughly

1 medium yellow or red onion, peeled and roughly chopped

1 medium tomato, coarsely chopped

1 (1-inch [2.5 cm]) piece ginger, peeled and finely chopped or grated

3 cloves garlic, peeled and finely chopped or grated

2 green Thai, serrano, or cayenne chiles, stems removed, finely chopped

1 tablespoon (15 mL) cumin seeds

1 teaspoon (5 mL) turmeric powder

1 teaspoon (5 mL) red chile powder

1 heaping tablespoon (20 mL) sea salt

9 cups (2.13 L) water

1. Put the lentils, onion, tomato, ginger, garlic, green chiles, cumin, turmeric, red chile powder, sea salt, and water in the slow cooker.

2. Cook on high for 8 hours. When it's done, pulse with an immersion blender until smooth. If you prefer a *dal* with some texture, reserve 1 cup, blend the rest, and then stir the reserved cup into the blended portion.

Try This! Serve to your kids as Little Dippers! I cut toasted *naan* into strips with a pizza cutter and serve with a bowl of this *dal*. They dip the *naan* in the *dal* and eat it up.

To make this dish in a 3½-quart slow cooker, halve all the ingredients and proceed with the recipe. A half recipe makes 5 cups (1.18 L).

Split Green Lentil and Rice Porridge

Moong Dal Chilkha Kitchari | SLOW COOKER SIZE: **5-QUART** • COOKING TIME: **3½ HOURS ON HIGH** • YIELD: **11 CUPS (2.60 L)**

In India, if you have an upset stomach or just want something comforting to eat, we don't reach for the chicken noodle soup, we make *kitchari*. Simply translated, the word means "all mixed up." In this one-pot meal, the lentils are mixed with the rice. To soothe an ailing stomach, the dish is made without spices and served with nourishing savory yogurt on the side. In my father's village, they would spice the dish up with lots of chiles and *ghee* and serve it as a treat for weekend lunches.

This is my cousin Juhi's favorite *kitchari* recipe. I love how simple it is.

2 cups (402 g) dried, split green lentils with skin, cleaned and washed thoroughly

1 cup (201 g) uncooked white basmati or brown rice, washed thoroughly

1 (4-inch [10 cm]) piece ginger, peeled and grated or ground in a food processor

2 tablespoons (30 mL) sea salt

1 teaspoon (5 mL) turmeric powder

1 pinch ajwain (carom) seeds

8 cups (1.89 L) water

1. Put lentils, rice, ginger, sea salt, turmeric, *ajwain*, and water in the slow cooker.

2. Cook on high for 3½ hours. Serve with plain yogurt and spicy Indian pickle (*achaar*) on the side.

Try This! Jazz this up by throwing in a chopped onion and a diced tomato with the other ingredients.

To make this dish in a 3½-quart slow cooker, halve all the ingredients and proceed with the recipe. A half recipe makes 6 cups (1.42 L).

Whole Green Lentil and Brown Rice Porridge

Sabut Moong Kitchari | SLOW COOKER SIZE: **5-QUART** • COOKING TIME: **5 HOURS ON HIGH** • YIELD: **10 CUPS (2.37 L)**

From the moment they could eat rice, I fed my girls brown rather than white. They eventually developed a taste for the whole-grain version. Cooked in a slow cooker with lentils, brown rice finishes cooking surprisingly quickly and tastes surprisingly good.

2 cups (402 g) whole dried moong dal with skin, cleaned and washed thoroughly

1 cup (201 g) brown rice, washed thoroughly

1 small yellow onion, peeled and finely chopped

1 medium tomato, finely chopped

1 (1-inch [2.5 cm]) piece ginger, peeled and finely chopped or grated

1 clove garlic, peeled and finely chopped or grated

2 green Thai chiles, stems removed, finely chopped

1 tablespoon (15 mL) cumin seeds

2 tablespoons (30 mL) sea salt

1 teaspoon (5 mL) turmeric powder

1 teaspoon (5 mL) red chile powder

8 cups (1.89 L) water

Butter, to serve

1 tablespoon (15 mL) finely chopped cilantro, for garnish

1 tablespoon (15 mL) peeled and finely chopped yellow, red, or white onion, for garnish

1. Put the lentils, rice, yellow onion, tomato, ginger, garlic, green chiles, cumin, sea salt, turmeric, red chile powder, and water in the slow cooker.

2. Cook on high for 5 hours.

3. To serve, spoon into bowls and top each serving with a pat of butter, a pinch of fresh cilantro, and the finely chopped onions.

To make this dish in a 3½-quart slow cooker, halve all the ingredients and proceed with the recipe. A half recipe makes 5 cups (1.18 L).

Dry Spiced Dal

Sooki Dal | SLOW COOKER SIZE: **3½-QUART** • COOKING TIME: **2½ HOURS ON HIGH** • YIELD: **7 CUPS (1.66 L)**

This is one of my husband's two favorite dishes. Whenever we visit my mother in Philadelphia, she always has a batch ready and waiting for him. It's a good thing I figured out how to make it in the slow cooker, because I could never be bothered to learn to make it on the stovetop (and he never forgets to remind me of this).

3 cups (603 g) dried, split, and skinned yellow moong dal or split and skinned urad dal, cleaned and washed thoroughly

1 small onion, peeled and finely chopped

1 (1-inch [2.5 cm]) piece ginger, peeled and grated

2–3 cloves garlic, peeled and minced or grated

1 teaspoon (5 mL) cumin seeds

1 teaspoon (5 mL) turmeric powder

1 tablespoon (15 mL) sea salt

3 cups (710 mL) water

1 tablespoon (15 mL) chopped fresh cilantro

Chopped green chiles, for garnish (optional)

Chopped onions, for garnish (optional)

1. Put the lentils, onion, ginger, garlic, cumin, turmeric, sea salt, and water in the slow cooker.

2. Cook on high for 2 hours, stirring once or twice. Check to see if the water has been absorbed. If not, cook for another 30 minutes until no liquid remains.

3. Garnish with the cilantro, chopped green chiles, and onions. Serve with *roti* or *naan* and spicy *achaar*.

Try This! This *dal* makes an excellent, protein-rich filling for wraps. Spread a tablespoon of hummus and then a tablespoon of *sooki dal* on a flour tortilla. Add any veggies you like, roll, and serve. You can also make this into a healthy side salad by adding 1 cup of cooked *dal* to 1 cup of chopped greens. Add mushrooms, and it's even better.

This recipe can be made in a 4-quart or 5-quart slow cooker using the same measurements.

Yellow Split-Pea Soup with Burnt Onions and Yogurt

SLOW COOKER SIZE: **5-QUART** • COOKING TIME: **4 HOURS ON HIGH** • YIELD: **10 CUPS (2.37 L)**

I describe this soup as spring in a spoon. It's sweet, refreshing, and deceptively easy to make. The taste is just a bit sweeter than its green counterpart, and the bright yellow color of this soup is a welcome change to ring in the warm months of the year—we seem to have too few of them in Chicago!

This is not a traditional Indian recipe, but I do add a very Indian twist in the form of burnt onions and savory *raita*.

3 cups (603 g) dried and skinned yellow split peas, cleaned and washed thoroughly

1 medium yellow or white onion, peeled and coarsely chopped

9 cups (2.13 L) water

1 tablespoon (15 mL) sea salt, plus more to taste

½ cup (100 g) burnt onions (instructions follow)

1 cup (236 mL) plain Greek yogurt

Black pepper to taste

1 teaspoon (5 mL) ground, roasted cumin

1. Place the dried peas, onion, water, and 1 tablespoon of sea salt in the slow cooker.

2. Cook on high for 3½ hours. Reserve 1 cup of the soup, and using an immersion blender, puree the rest. (Alternatively, you can blend in batches in a regular blender.) Return the reserved cup of soup and cook everything for another 30 minutes.

3. In a small bowl, whisk together the yogurt, sea salt and black pepper to taste, and cumin.

4. To serve, place a cup of the soup in a bowl and top with a teaspoon of the burnt onions and a teaspoon (5 mL) of the yogurt mixture.

Try This! Burnt onions are so fun to make and eat. Finely chop 1 medium yellow or red onion. Heat 2 tablespoons (30 mL) canola oil, vegetable oil, butter, or *ghee*. Once the oil is hot, add the onions and cook until completely burnt and crisp. Stir frequently so it doesn't stick. Store in the refrigerator for up to a week.

To make this dish in a 3½-quart slow cooker, halve all the ingredients and proceed with the recipe. A half recipe makes 5 cups (1.18 L).

Indian-Inspired Vegetable Soup

SLOW COOKER SIZE: **5-QUART** • COOKING TIME: **7 HOURS ON HIGH** • YIELD: **14 CUPS (3.31 L)**

My mom makes the most amazing vegetable soups. This recipe is a great example of how she blends fresh vegetables with Indian lentils and spices. You may substitute any vegetables you have on hand, such as cauliflower, spinach, or broccoli. You can also try using barley or wild rice as the grain, and substituting another lentil for the *moong dal.*

2 yellow or white onions, peeled and chopped

2 large tomatoes, chopped

1 (2-inch [5 cm]) piece ginger, peeled and minced or grated

3 cloves garlic, peeled and chopped or grated

4 large carrots, peeled and chopped

4 stalks celery, chopped

½ head green cabbage, chopped

2 tablespoons (30 mL) dried whole moong dal with skin

2 tablespoons (30 mL) brown rice

2 tablespoons (30 mL) quinoa

1 tablespoon (15 mL) cumin seeds

½ teaspoon (2 mL) turmeric powder

Sea salt and pepper to taste

Shredded cheese (any kind), for garnish

Crushed tortilla chips, for garnish

1. Put all the ingredients in slow cooker. Cover with water to about 2 inches above the contents.

2. Cook on high for 7 hours. Once it's cooked, blend a few times with an immersion blender or take out 3 cups, process in a blender, and return it to the slow cooker.

3. Add sea salt and pepper to taste. Garnish with a pinch of shredded cheese and crushed tortilla chips.

To make this dish in a 3½-quart slow cooker, halve all the ingredients and proceed with the recipe. A half recipe makes 7 cups (1.66 L).

Your Notes ...

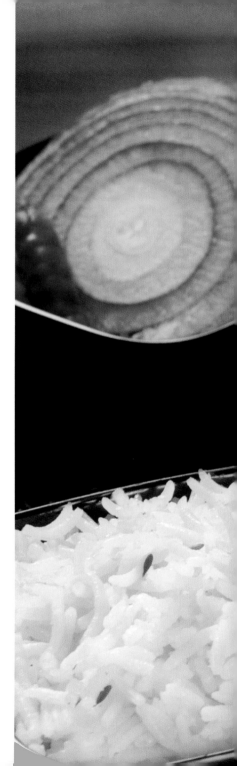

Beans
& Peas

"I like to buy mine dried rather than in cans because dried are cheaper and also break down better during the cooking process."

Punjabi Curried Kidney Beans

Punjabi Curried Kidney Beans

Rajmah | SLOW COOKER SIZE: **5-QUART** • COOKING TIME: **11 HOURS ON HIGH** • YIELD: **10 CUPS (2.37 L)**

Rajmah, a North Indian version of chili or red beans and rice, is the quintessential comfort food for Punjabis. Ask anyone from that region, and she'll tell you she grew up eating these hearty beans over rice in her home as a quick Sunday lunch or in her college hostel.

It's not a dish that's usually considered refined enough to be served in a restaurant, but it is a classic. It's even better when served over a bed of rice with some savory, tangy yogurt on the side.

I remember one buddy in graduate school at the University of Hawaii who had just arrived from India and was so desperate to eat *rajmah* that he substituted ketchup for tomatoes. I wouldn't recommend such shortcuts, nor would I recommend using canned beans or cream, as some recipes suggest. Keep it simple, and I guarantee you'll make this dish over and over again.

3 cups (603 g) dried red kidney beans, cleaned and washed thoroughly

1 medium yellow or red onion, peeled and roughly chopped

2 medium tomatoes, diced

1 (2-inch [5 cm]) piece ginger, peeled and chopped or grated

3 cloves garlic, peeled and chopped or grated

4–6 green Thai, serrano, or cayenne chiles, stems removed, chopped

3 whole cloves

1 (2–4 inch [5–10 cm]) cinnamon stick

1 tablespoon (15 mL) cumin seeds

1 tablespoon (15 mL) red chile powder

2 tablespoons (30 mL) sea salt

1 teaspoon (5 mL) turmeric powder

1 teaspoon (5 mL) garam masala

9 cups (2.13 L) water

½ cup (100 g) chopped fresh cilantro

1. Put the kidney beans, onion, tomatoes, ginger, garlic, green chiles, cloves, cinnamon stick, cumin, red chile powder, sea salt, turmeric, *garam masala*, and water in the slow cooker.

2. Cook on high for 11 hours, until the beans break down and become somewhat creamy.

3. Remove and discard the cloves (if you can find them!) and cinnamon stick. If the *rajmah* is not creamy enough, take an immersion blender and press it two or three times to break up some of the beans. If using a blender, take out about 1 cup (237 mL) and process in the blender, then return it to the slow cooker. Be careful not to process all of the beans; most of them should remain whole.

4. Stir in the cilantro. Serve over a bed of basmati or brown rice with a side of *raita* and an Indian salad.

Try This! After cooking, turn off the slow cooker and add 1 cup (237 mL) plain yogurt. Stir well and let the slow cooker sit with the lid on for about 10 minutes. This adds a unique tang.

To make this dish in a 3½ quart slow cooker, halve all the ingredients and proceed with the recipe. A half recipe makes 5 cups (1.18 L).

Dad's Rajmah

SLOW COOKER SIZE: **5-QUART** • COOKING TIME: **10 HOURS ON HIGH, 2 HOURS ON LOW** • YIELD: **10 CUPS (2.37 L)**

My father grew up in Bhikhi, a small village surrounded by fields of mustard greens and wheat in the northern agricultural state of Punjab in India. The residents of the region love their food fresh, spicy, and dripping with *ghee*. Most work so hard in the fields that butter is not considered a health hazard. In fact, villagers are encouraged to eat as much butter as possible to increase their physical strength.

Though he raised a family in the United States, my father never lost his taste for authentic and spicy Indian foods. This is his recipe for *rajmah*. Don't be intimidated by all the chile peppers and garlic. They are tempered as the beans break down into a fabulously creamy base.

Skeptical at first, I did ask Dad to verify the amount of chile and all he said was, "for spicy people, it's no big deal." So, if you are one of these "spicy people" or just like an adventure, try this recipe. Just keep a cold drink handy.

3 cups (603 g) dried red kidney beans, cleaned and washed thoroughly

1 medium yellow or red onion, peeled and chopped

1 (2-inch [5 cm]) piece ginger, peeled and chopped

12 cloves garlic, peeled and chopped

8–10 green Thai, serrano, or cayenne chiles, stems removed, chopped

¼ cup (59 mL) tomato paste

2 tablespoons (30 mL) cumin seeds

2 tablespoons (30 mL) sea salt

2 teaspoons (10 mL) turmeric powder

2 teaspoons (10 mL) red chile powder

4 tablespoons (60 mL) unsalted butter

12 cups (2.84 L) water

2 tablespoons (30 mL) fresh cilantro, chopped

1. Put the kidney beans, onion, ginger, garlic, green chiles, tomato paste, cumin, sea salt, turmeric, red chile powder, butter, and water in the slow cooker.

2. Cook on high for 10 hours. Turn the slow cooker to low and cook for another 2 hours.

3. When it's done cooking, add the cilantro.

4. Serve over basmati or brown rice with a plate of raw onions doused with fresh lemon juice and *raita* on the side.

To make this dish in a 3½-quart slow cooker, halve all the ingredients and proceed with the recipe. A half recipe makes 5 cups (1.18 L).

Curried Chickpeas

Rasa walla Kabuli Chana | SLOW COOKER SIZE: **5-QUART** • COOKING TIME: **14 HOURS ON HIGH** • YIELD: **13 CUPS (3.08 L)**

Like *rajmah*, this dish is a staple in virtually every North Indian home—and for a good reason. It's delicious and filling. It's also a great non-meat protein alternative for many Indians—vegetarians and meat eaters alike.

The key to making this dish authentic is to include a hint of tartness. The spice blend, **chana masala**, is critical because in addition to the basic spices, it also incorporates mango and pomegranate powders for a slightly sour taste. This slightly soupy dish is a perfect comfort food after a long day at work.

3 cups (603 g) dried chickpeas, cleaned and washed thoroughly

1 medium yellow or red onion, peeled and finely chopped

1 medium tomato, diced

1 (2-inch [5 cm]) piece ginger, peeled and chopped or grated

4 cloves garlic, peeled and chopped, minced, or grated

4–6 green Thai, serrano, or cayenne chiles, stems removed, chopped

1 tablespoon (15 mL) cumin seeds

1 tablespoon (15 mL) ground coriander

1 tablespoon (15 mL) garam masala

1 tablespoon (15 mL) chana masala

1 tablespoon (15 mL) red chile powder

2 tablespoons (30 mL) sea salt

1 teaspoon (5 mL) turmeric powder

12 cups (2.84 L) water

2 tablespoons (30 mL) fresh cilantro, chopped

Thinly sliced red onion, for garnish

Lime wedges, for garnish

1. Put the chickpeas, onion, tomato, ginger, garlic, green chiles, cumin, coriander, *garam masala*, *chana masala*, red chile powder, sea salt, turmeric, and water in the slow cooker.

2. Cook on high for 14 hours. Toward the end of cooking time, use the back of a large spoon to mash some of the beans against the walls of the slow cooker or pulse 2 or 3 times with an immersion blender. Add the cilantro.

3. To serve, sprinkle sliced onions on top and eat with a lime wedge on the side accompanied by *roti* or *naan*, or in a bowl over basmati or brown rice.

Try This! Toast a hamburger bun. Place a slice of cheese (any kind) on each half of the bun and heap on a spoonful of *chana* and fresh, diced onions. It's a fast and healthy veggie alternative to the open-faced sandwich. My kids love this as a snack. For them, I like to use mini whole-wheat dinner rolls.

To make this dish in a 3½-quart slow cooker, halve all the ingredients and proceed with the recipe. A half recipe makes 6 cups (1.42 L).

Amla Chickpeas

Sooka Amla Chana | SLOW COOKER SIZE: **5-QUART** • COOKING TIME: **7 HOURS ON HIGH** • YIELD: **14 CUPS (3.31 L)**

My father's sister (*Shiela bua*) in London showed me how to make this dish, and I can't stop making it—it's so delicious. The key is to darken the chickpeas during the cooking process by using dried *amla*—an Indian gooseberry. Any Indian grocer will carry them, but if you don't have any on hand, just use black tea bags. The *amla* is worth tracking down because it will infuse your dish with vitamin C.

The amount of water added to the slow cooker should be limited so that the result is a dry bean dish. Because of this, it helps to mix the beans a few times during the cooking process to prevent the top layer from drying out. If it does, just skim it off and discard before adding other ingredients.

6 cups (1.2 kg) dried chickpeas, cleaned and washed thoroughly

10–15 pieces dried whole amla

8 cups (1.89 L) water

1 medium yellow or red onion, peeled and sliced into thin strips

1 medium tomato, sliced

1 (2-inch [5 cm]) piece ginger, peeled and cut into thin 1-inch (2.5 cm) strips

4 cloves garlic, peeled and chopped or grated

4–6 green Thai, serrano, or cayenne chiles, stems removed, chopped

2 tablespoons (30 mL) chana masala

1 tablespoon (15 mL) red chile powder

2 tablespoons (30 mL) sea salt

1 teaspoon (5 mL) turmeric powder

1 tablespoon (15 mL) cumin seeds

½ cup (125 mL) vegetable or canola oil

Juice of 1 large lemon

2 tablespoons (30 mL) fresh cilantro, chopped

1. Place the chickpeas, *amla*, and water in the slow cooker. (If you substitute tea bags, remove and discard the paper, staple, and string attached to the bag, but be careful not to break the bag.)

2. Cook on high for 7 hours, ideally mixing 2 to 3 times to ensure that the top layer doesn't dry out. Remove the *amla* or tea bags. The chickpeas should be almost black in color.

3. Turn off the slow cooker. Using a spoon, make a shallow well in the top of the beans. Add the onion, tomato, ginger, garlic, chiles, *chana masala*, red chile powder, sea salt, turmeric, and cumin into the well. (The cumin should be added last so that it crackles when you add the oil.)

4. On the stovetop, warm the oil in a shallow pan over medium-high heat until it's so hot that steam starts to come off the top. (Be careful not to burn the oil.) The oil must be very hot, or it won't cook the fresh vegetables or spices in the dish. Working slowly and carefully (because the hot oil can splatter, especially once it hits the uncooked cumin), pour the oil onto the fresh ingredients in small circles so that everything is covered. Replace the lid in the slow cooker and allow the dish to sit for 10 to 15 minutes.

5. Add the lemon juice and cilantro, mix well, and serve with *roti* or *naan*. Lemon

juice sometimes offsets the sea salt in a recipe, so you might need to add a touch more sea salt before serving.

Try this! Stuff a spoonful of the beans into half a lightly toasted pita pocket. Drizzle salted yogurt (or *raita*) on top and garnish with finely chopped onions and tomatoes. My kids love making their own pita pockets. You can also opt to leave the *amla* in the dish— it'll just add another layer of tartness. If you don't like using canned chickpeas, make a batch of this without the *amla* and, once cooked, keep it in the fridge for homemade hummus or a protein-rich addition to salads.

Note: There have been occasions when I haven't had time to add the other ingredients into the chickpeas and instead have had to refrigerate them first. If you do this, be sure to reheat the beans on the stovetop before adding the garnish and hot oil. The dish just won't taste or blend the same way if you pour the hot oil over cold beans. Remember that manufacturers recommend not reheating food in a slow cooker.

To make this dish in a 3½-quart slow cooker, halve all the ingredients and proceed with the recipe. A half recipe makes 7 cups (1.66 L).

Tangy Tamarind Chickpeas

Khata Imlee Chana | SLOW COOKER SIZE: **5-QUART** • COOKING TIME: **12 HOURS ON HIGH**
YIELD: **14 CUPS (3.31 L)**

The tartness of this dish takes me back to eating freshly seasoned and spiced chickpeas along the lake in Chandigarh, India, the city where I was born and spent much of my childhood. Back then, my grandmother forbid us to eat street food, but my cousins and I never listened. Our stomachs suffered, but to this day I don't regret one bite.

6 cups (1.2 kg) dried chickpeas, cleaned and washed thoroughly

11 cups (2.60 L) water

1 large yellow or red onion, peeled and chopped

1 (2-inch [5 cm]) piece ginger, peeled and chopped

20 cloves garlic, peeled

8 green Thai, serrano, or cayenne chiles

2 tablespoons (30 mL) ground cumin

2 tablespoons (30 mL) ground coriander

1 tablespoon (15 mL) red chile powder

4 tablespoons (60 mL) thick yogurt (I use Greek)

2 tablespoons (30 mL) garam masala

2 heaping tablespoons (40 mL) tamarind paste

2 tablespoons (30 mL) sea salt

½ lemon, seeded

Sliced red onion, for topping

1. Place the chickpeas and water in the slow cooker.

2. In a food processor, puree the onion, ginger, garlic, green chiles, cumin, coriander, red chile powder, yogurt, *garam masala*, tamarind paste, and sea salt, and add to the slow cooker. Cook on high for 10 hours.

3. Add the half lemon and cook another 2 hours on high. After cooking, remove and discard the lemon.

4. Top with the sliced red onions.

5. Serve with piping hot, thick *naan*.

To make this dish in a 3½-quart slow cooker, halve all the ingredients and proceed with the recipe. A half recipe makes 7 cups (1.66 L).

Black Chickpea Curry

Kaala Chana | SLOW COOKER SIZE: **5-QUART** • COOKING TIME: **9 HOURS ON HIGH** • YIELD: **13 CUPS (3.075 L)**

These chickpeas are nothing like their white counterparts. They are smaller, brownish black in color, and extremely thick-skinned. They have a warm, earthy flavor that I sometimes prefer over white chickpeas. My father always laughs when he hears that my kids have been eating this for dinner. He says that in his day, they fed horses black chickpeas because they are so high in protein, and that my kids will be as tough as stallions. That remains to be seen.

This bean has such a tough skin that even after hours of cooking it doesn't break down on its own. When I was younger, I ate it over rice and loved the flavor-infused, soupy part of the dish so much that I'd discard the heavy beans that sank to the bottom of my bowl. To keep your own kids from doing this, I recommend mashing some of the beans with a large spoon at the end of the cooking process.

3 cups (603 g) dried black chickpeas, cleaned and washed thoroughly

1 medium yellow or red onion, peeled and quartered

1 medium tomato, quartered

1 (2-inch [5 cm]) piece ginger, peeled and roughly chopped

4 cloves garlic, peeled

4–6 green Thai, serrano, or cayenne chiles, stems removed

1 tablespoon (15 mL) cumin seeds

1 teaspoon (5 mL) turmeric powder

1 teaspoon (5 mL) red chile powder

2 tablespoons (30 mL) sea salt

7 cups (1.66 L) water

2 tablespoons (30 mL) cilantro

2 tablespoons (30 mL) lemon juice

1. Place the black chickpeas in the slow cooker.

2. In a food processor, puree the onion, tomato, ginger, garlic, and green chiles into a paste. Add this mixture to the slow cooker.

3. Add the cumin, turmeric, red chile powder, sea salt, and water to the slow cooker.

4. Cook on high for 9 hours.

5. Using the back of a spoon, an immersion blender, or a regular blender, mash about a third of the beans.

6. Add the cilantro and lemon juice. Serve with steaming bowls of basmati or brown rice.

To make this dish in a 3½-quart slow cooker, halve all the ingredients and proceed with the recipe. A half recipe makes 7 cups (1.66 L).

Dry, Tangy Black Chickpeas

Sooka, Khata Kaala Chana | SLOW COOKER SIZE: **5-QUART** • COOKING TIME: **3 HOURS ON HIGH, 1 HOUR ON LOW** • YIELD: **13 CUPS (3.08 L)**

There are hundreds of Hindu festivals and just as many special foods associated with those celebrations. Dried, spicy, sour black chickpeas are considered especially auspicious when eaten with round, fried *puris* and sweet halwa. The sweet-spicy combination is amazing.

6 cups (1.2 kg) dried black chickpeas, cleaned and washed thoroughly

7 black cardamom pods

7 cups (1.66 L) water

2 tablespoons (30 mL) vegetable or canola oil

1 tablespoon (15 mL) shyah jeera

1 large yellow or red onion, peeled and finely chopped

4 cloves garlic, peeled and minced, grated, or chopped

1 (2-inch [5 cm]) piece ginger, peeled and grated or chopped

2 tomatoes, diced

4–6 green Thai, serrano, or cayenne chiles, stems removed, halved lengthwise

1 tablespoon (15 mL) garam masala

1 tablespoon (15 mL) mango powder

2 tablespoons (30 mL) sea salt

1 teaspoon (5 mL) turmeric powder

1 teaspoon (5 mL) red chile powder

Juice of 1 large lemon

1 large bunch cilantro, chopped

1. Put the chickpeas, cardamom, and water in the slow cooker. Cook on high for 3 hours. Mix a few times during the cooking process to make sure the top layer of beans does not dry out. When the beans are done, very little water should be left in the slow cooker, and the beans should be soft and easy to bite. Remember, black chickpeas won't break down, but they should not be hard. If they are still tough, cook another 30 minutes to an hour, adding about ½ cup boiling water if needed.

2. Warm the oil in a frying pan over medium-high heat. Once it's hot, add the *shyah jeera*. When that sizzles, add the onion. Cook, stirring, for 2 to 3 minutes. Add the garlic and ginger and cook for another minute or two. Add this mixture to the slow cooker along with the tomatoes, green chiles, *garam masala*, mango powder, sea salt, turmeric, and red chile powder.

3. Turn the slow cooker to low and cook for another hour.

4. Once the chickpeas are finished cooking, remove and discard the cardamom pods and add the lemon juice and cilantro. Serve with *puris*, *roti*, or *naan*.

To make this dish in a 3½-quart slow cooker, halve all the ingredients and proceed with the recipe. A half recipe makes 6 cups (1.42 L).

Chickpea Curry with Fresh Dill Leaves

Rasa walla Kabuli Chana | SLOW COOKER SIZE: **5-QUART** • COOKING TIME: **10 HOURS ON HIGH** • YIELD: **14 CUPS (3.31 L)**

This dish can be made with white chickpeas or with split and skinned Indian chickpeas called *chana dal.* I was inspired to try this in a slow cooker after seeing it in Ruta Kahate's *5 Spices, 50 Dishes.* It's a nice alternative to all the other heavily spiced and aromatic chickpea dishes that normally make up the North Indian diet.

6 cups (1.2 kg) dried chickpeas, cleaned and washed thoroughly

1 medium yellow onion, peeled and finely chopped

1 (2-inch [5 cm]) piece ginger, peeled and grated

4 cloves garlic, peeled and minced, grated, or chopped

2 green Thai, serrano, or cayenne chiles, stems removed, chopped

1 teaspoon (5 mL) ground cumin

1 teaspoon (5 mL) ground coriander

1 teaspoon (5 mL) turmeric powder

1 teaspoon (5 mL) red chile powder

1 heaping tablespoon (20 mL) sea salt

11 cups (2.60 L) water

3 cups (603 g) finely chopped fresh dill leaves (about 2 bunches)

1. Put the chickpeas, onion, ginger, garlic, green chiles, cumin, coriander, turmeric, red chile powder, sea salt, and water in the slow cooker. Cook on high for 9½ hours.

2. Add the dill and cook for another 30 minutes. Enjoy with *roti* or *naan* or stuffed in a pita pocket.

To make this dish in a 3½-quart slow cooker, halve all the ingredients and proceed with the recipe. A half recipe makes 7 cups (1.66 L).

Goan Black-Eyed Peas

SLOW COOKER SIZE: **5-QUART** • COOKING TIME: **7 HOURS ON HIGH** • YIELD: **14 CUPS (3.31 L)**

In our North Indian home, we never cooked with coconut milk so I never ate this dish growing up. I was inspired to try it in my slow cooker after seeing it in Ruta Kahate's *5 Spices, 50 Dishes*. Just reading her story about eating this with bread in the mornings in Goa inspired me to make it for dinner, and now you can too.

3 cups (603 g) dried black-eyed peas, cleaned and washed thoroughly

2 small tomatoes

1 large yellow onion, peeled and cut into large pieces

1 (2-inch [5 cm]) piece ginger, peeled and cut into large pieces

2 cloves garlic, peeled

4–6 green Thai, serrano, or cayenne chiles

2 tablespoons (30 mL) ground coriander

2 tablespoons (30 mL) sea salt

1 teaspoon (5 mL) turmeric powder

1 teaspoon (5 mL) ground cumin

1 tablespoon (15 mL) brown sugar

9 cups (2.13 L) water

1 (14-oz [414 mL]) can regular or light coconut milk

Fresh cilantro, for garnish

1. Put the black-eyed peas in slow cooker.

2. Bring a pot of water to a boil on the stovetop. Cut an X into the non-stem end of each tomato with a sharp knife and add the tomatoes to the boiling water. Cook for about 2 minutes, or until the peel starts to curl back. Pull the tomatoes out of the water with tongs, allow them to cool, and peel them. Roughly chop the tomatoes.

3. Grind the tomatoes, onion, ginger, garlic, and chiles in a food processor. Add this mixture to the slow cooker along with the coriander, sea salt, turmeric, ground cumin, brown sugar, and water. Cook on high for 7 hours.

4. About 10 minutes before the cooking time ends, stir in the coconut milk. Replace the lid and continue cooking for 10 minutes.

5. Garnish with cilantro. Serve with bread, *naan*, or rice, or on its own as a soup.

To make this dish in a 3½-quart slow cooker, halve all the ingredients and proceed with the recipe. A half recipe makes 7 cups (1.66 L).

Cilantro-Infused Black-Eyed Peas

Dhania Waale Lobhia | SLOW COOKER SIZE: **5-QUART** • COOKING TIME: **10 HOURS ON HIGH** • YIELD: **14 CUPS (3.31 L)**

One thing my husband and I can agree on is that we did not enjoy eating black-eyed peas growing up. Both our mothers made it with the traditional tomato-based curry. I was on a mission to change this traditional recipe around a bit and create a dish we could all enjoy eating. And I did it! The first time I served these cilantro-infused beans to my family they all loved them—including my husband.

3 cups (603 g) dried black-eyed peas, cleaned and washed thoroughly

2 medium tomatoes

1 medium yellow or red onion, peeled and roughly chopped

1 (2-inch [5 cm]) piece ginger, peeled and cut in small pieces

4 cloves garlic, peeled

2–3 green Thai, serrano, or cayenne chiles, stems removed

2 large bunches fresh cilantro (about 2 cups [402 g]), separated

2 tablespoons (30 mL) roasted cumin and coriander mixture (see page 27)

2 tablespoons (30 mL) sea salt

1 teaspoon (5 mL) turmeric powder

1 teaspoon (5 mL) red chile powder

6 cups (1.42 L) water

1. Put the black-eyed peas in the slow cooker.

2. Bring a pot of water to a boil on the stovetop. Cut an X into the non-stem end of each tomato with a sharp knife and add the tomatoes to the boiling water. Cook for about 2 minutes, or until the peel starts to curl back. Pull the tomatoes out of the water with tongs, allow them to cool, and peel them. Roughly chop the tomatoes.

3. Put the tomatoes, onion, ginger, garlic, green chiles, and 1 cup (237 mL) of the cilantro in a food processor and grind until smooth. Add this mixture to the slow cooker.

4. Add the cumin and coriander mixture, sea salt, turmeric, red chile powder, and water. Cook on high for 10 hours.

5. Turn off the slow cooker and add the remaining 1 cup (237 mL) chopped cilantro. Serve over a steaming bowl of basmati or brown rice or with *roti* or *naan*.

To make this dish in a 3½-quart slow cooker, halve all the ingredients and proceed with the recipe. A half recipe makes 7 cups (1.66 L).

Your Notes ...

Vegetables

"*Aloo Baingan* is the first recipe I ever cooked. It was taught to me by my paternal grandfather, a landowner from a small village in India. He insisted on putting the woody stems of the eggplant into the dish."

Fiery Eggplant

Spiced Cauliflower and Potatoes

Aloo Gobi | SLOW COOKER SIZE: **4- OR 5-QUART** • COOKING TIME: **3 HOURS ON LOW** • YIELD: **7 CUPS (1.66 L)**

Until I made this myself in the slow cooker, I refused to believe my mother-in-law when she said it was possible. I also wondered why I wouldn't just make this dish on the stovetop, where it could sit for less time. After trying it once, I realized the answer: because I can now stick it in my slow cooker and go about my day. I don't think twice about the kids near the stove or anything burning.

My father—the real foodie of the family—also wouldn't believe this dish could be made well in the slow cooker, so he just had to try it himself. He had me on the phone in excitement for half an hour after trying it for the first time. He insists on the tomato. I like it better without. You be the judge.

1 large cauliflower, washed and cut into 1-inch pieces (about 8 cups/1.89 L)

1 large potato (russet or yellow), peeled and diced (about 2 cups/473 mL)

1 medium yellow or red onion, peeled and coarsely chopped

1 medium tomato, diced (optional)

1 (2-inch [5 cm]) piece ginger, peeled and grated

3 cloves garlic, peeled and chopped, minced, or grated

3–4 green Thai, serrano, or cayenne chiles, stems removed, chopped or sliced lengthwise

1 tablespoon (15 mL) cumin seeds

1 tablespoon (15 mL) red chile powder

1 tablespoon (15 mL) garam masala

1 tablespoon (15 mL) sea salt

1 teaspoon (5 mL) turmeric powder

3 tablespoons (50 mL) vegetable or canola oil

1 heaping tablespoon (20 mL) fresh cilantro, chopped

1. Put all the ingredients except the cilantro in the slow cooker. Mix well.

2. Cook on low for 3 hours. Mix once or twice during cooking, especially in the beginning. Eventually the cauliflower will release enough liquid to prevent anything from sticking to the sides of the slow cooker.

3. Add cilantro. Mix well but gently so as not to break up the cauliflower. Serve with *roti* or *naan* and a side of onion and cucumber salad.

To make this dish in a 3½-quart slow cooker, halve all the ingredients and proceed with the recipe. A half recipe makes 4 cups (946 mL).

Spicy Punjabi Eggplant with Potatoes

Aloo Baingan | SLOW COOKER SIZE: **4- OR 5-QUART** • COOKING TIME: **5 HOURS ON LOW** • YIELD: **7 CUPS (1.66 L)**

Aloo baingan is the first recipe I ever learned to cook and the only one my paternal grandfather demonstrated for me. He was a land-owner from a small village in Punjab and a huge foodie. He loved to super-vise the cooking in the family *haveli* (communal home) and to eat wonder-fully fragrant, authentically spiced Indian foods.

I still remember him insisting on putting the green woody stems of the eggplant into the dish because, he said, if you threw it away, the sweet, succulent meat inside would also be discarded. While eating, he'd pull out the cooked stems and suck the sweet meat out.

With this dish, I've made eggplant lovers out of many friends and neigh-bors who had previously written the vegetable off. Then again, they'd never had it prepared quite this way.

3 medium eggplants, diced (about 12 cups/2.5 kg)

1 large potato (russet or yellow), peeled and diced (about 2 cups/402 g)

1 medium yellow or red onion, peeled and roughly chopped

1 (2 inch [5 cm]) piece ginger, peeled and cut into 1½-inch (3 cm) matchsticks

6 cloves garlic, peeled and coarsely chopped

3–4 green Thai, serrano, or cayenne chiles, stems removed, chopped or sliced lengthwise

1 tablespoon (15 mL) cumin seeds

1 tablespoon (15 mL) red chile powder

1 tablespoon (15 mL) garam masala

1 teaspoon (5 mL) turmeric powder

¼ cup (59 mL) vegetable or canola oil

2 tablespoons (30 mL) sea salt

2 tablespoons (30 mL) fresh cilantro, chopped

1. Put the eggplant, potato, onion, ginger, garlic, green chiles, cumin, red chile powder, *garam masala*, turmeric, and oil in the slow cooker. Cook on low for 3 hours.

2. Remove the lid and cook for another 2 hours. This will help dry up some of the moisture released by the eggplant during the cooking process.

3. Add the sea salt and cilantro. (Sea salt is better added in the end because it will cause the eggplant to sweat and release more water if added earlier). Serve with *roti* or *naan*. This is also good stuffed inside a pita pocket.

To make this dish in a 3½-quart slow cooker, halve all the ingredients and proceed with the recipe. A half recipe makes 4 cups (946 mL).

Spicy Butternut Squash

Paitha | SLOW COOKER SIZE: **4- OR 5-QUART** • COOKING TIME: **4 HOURS ON LOW** • YIELD: **5 CUPS (1.2 L)**

The Indian take on squash is out of this world. It's a crazy mix of salty, spicy, and sweet, with a hint of tart. The first time I learned how to make this dish successfully was in Hawaii, as a graduate student at the East West Center from my fellow foodie – Mukta. My mom helped adapt it from stovetop to slow cooker.

2 tablespoons (30 mL) vegetable or canola oil

2 teaspoons (10 mL) fenugreek seeds

2 teaspoons (10 mL) cumin seeds

2 black cardamom pods

1 (2-inch [5 cm]) cinnamon stick

1 yellow or red onion, peeled and chopped

1 medium tomato, finely chopped

2 teaspoons (10 mL) turmeric powder

1 teaspoon (5 mL) ground coriander

4 pounds (1.89 kg) butternut squash, peeled and cut into 1-inch (2.5 cm) pieces (about 8 cups)

3–4 green Thai, serrano, or cayenne chiles, stems removed, chopped or sliced lengthwise

2 teaspoons (10 mL) brown sugar

1 teaspoon (5 mL) garam masala

2 teaspoons (10 mL) sea salt

1 teaspoon (5 mL) red chile powder

1 tablespoon (15 mL) fresh lemon juice

1. Heat the oil in a saucepan over medium-high heat. Once it's hot, add the fenugreek, cumin, cardamom, and cinnamon stick. Cook 3 to 4 minutes, stirring constantly, until the mixture sizzles. Add the onion and cook for another minute or so, until the onion browns slightly. Add to slow cooker and turn it on high.

2. Add the tomato, turmeric, and coriander. Mix well.

3. After a few minutes, add the squash and mix very well. Allow to cook for a few more minutes. Turn the slow cooker to low and cook for 4 hours, stirring a few times during cooking.

4. Add the green chiles, brown sugar, *garam masala*, sea salt, red chile powder, and lemon juice. Mix well. Garnish with cilantro and serve with *roti* or *naan*.

To make this dish in a 3½-quart slow cooker, halve all the ingredients and proceed with the recipe. A half recipe makes 2 cups (478 mL).

Fenugreek-Laced Carrots

Methi Gajar | SLOW COOKER SIZE: **4- OR 5-QUART** • COOKING TIME: **4 HOURS ON HIGH** • YIELD: **5 CUPS (1.6 KG)**

I'm not sure why I'm obsessed with a carrot dish, but this one is absolutely heavenly. There's something about the sweetness of the carrots that just blends really well with the fenugreek.

In India, the carrots are even sweeter and are deep red in color. Here, we have no choice but to use those available at the local grocer. You'll still have a dish you'll want to make over and over again.

16 medium carrots, peeled and sliced in ½–1-inch (1.2–2.5 cm) thick round slices (about 8 cups [1.89 L])

1 (2-inch [5 cm]) piece ginger, peeled and grated

1 teaspoon (5 mL) turmeric powder

1 teaspoon (5 mL) garam masala

½ cup (100 g) dried fenugreek (methi) leaves

2 tablespoons (30 mL) vegetable or canola oil

1 teaspoon (5 mL) sea salt

1. Put the carrots, ginger, turmeric, *garam masala*, and fenugreek leaves in the slow cooker. Drizzle the oil over the vegetables. Cook on high for 4 hours.

2. Add the sea salt. Mix well and serve with *roti* or *naan*.

To make this dish in a 3½-quart slow cooker, halve all the ingredients and proceed with the recipe. A half recipe makes 2 cups (478 mL).

Mustard Greens with Spinach

Sarson ka Saag | SLOW COOKER SIZE: **5-QUART** • COOKING TIME: **6 HOURS ON HIGH, 1 HOUR ON LOW** • YIELD: **10 CUPS (2.37 L)**

This is a dish close to the hearts of most Punjabis. Everywhere you go in this rich agricultural state, you'll find bright green fields with yellow flowers where mustard greens have been planted. Bollywood actors dance through these fields in love scenes and sing about them longingly. Eating mustard greens is synonymous with being Punjabi.

This dish is surprisingly addictive. I often don't crave it for months, but when I make it, I can't get enough. I like balancing the strong taste of mustard by mixing it with spinach, but you could also make this dish with only mustard greens. Traditionally, it is served with corn *rotis*, or *makhi ki roti*, but you can serve it with any Indian bread.

1 pound (0.45 kg) mustard greens, trimmed and washed thoroughly

1 pound (0.45 kg) spinach, trimmed and washed thoroughly

1 large yellow or red onion, peeled and roughly chopped

1 (2-inch [5-cm]) piece ginger, peeled and chopped

15 cloves garlic, peeled

6–8 green Thai, serrano, or cayenne chiles, stems removed

1 tablespoon (15 mL) ground coriander

2 tablespoons (30 mL) corn meal

1½ tablespoons (22.5 mL) sea salt

1 teaspoon (5 mL) turmeric powder

2 cups (473 mL) water

1 teaspoon (5 mL) garam masala

1. Put the mustard greens, spinach, onion, ginger, garlic, green chiles, coriander, corn meal, sea salt, turmeric, and water in the slow cooker.

2. Cook on high for 6 hours. Blend until smooth with an immersion blender. If using regular blender, return the mixture to the slow cooker after processing.

3. Add the *garam masala*. Cook on low for another hour. Serve with corn *rotis*, regular *rotis*, or *naan*.

Try This! Pour the finished dish over a piece of freshly made cornbread. Yum!

To make this dish in a 3½-quart slow cooker, halve all the ingredients and proceed with the recipe. A half recipe makes 5 cups (1.18 L).

Curried Spinach with Homemade Cheese

Palak Paneer | SLOW COOKER SIZE: **5-QUART** • COOKING TIME: **3 HOURS ON HIGH, 2 HOURS ON LOW** • YIELD: **10 CUPS (2.37 L) WITH CHEESE**

This dish needs no introduction. Anyone who has ever had Indian food has tasted *palak paneer* and loved it. I'm now here to tell you that it's a cinch to make in the slow cooker. The best thing about making it at home is that you forego the oil and cream that overwhelm rather than enhance the amazing flavors in this dish.

Unfortunately, *paneer* is still best made on the stovetop. But with my recipe on page 98, you'll be a pro the first time you try it. Your friends will be amazed. If you don't have the time, just purchase it. Many grocery stores carry *paneer* in the refrigerated section, but the cheapest and freshest is always that purchased from an Indian grocer.

Don't worry about drying the spinach after you wash it. The excess water actually prevents the spinach from drying out in the beginning of the cooking process. Also, the amount of spinach may look like it's too much, but trust me—even if you have to cram the lid of the slow cooker down at first. Spinach lets off so much water that it will cook down eventually and you'll have plenty of extra room.

---

2 pounds (1 kg) fresh spinach, washed thoroughly

2 large yellow or red onion, peeled and roughly chopped

3 medium tomatoes, roughly chopped

1 (4-inch [10 cm]) piece ginger, peeled and roughly chopped

20 cloves garlic, peeled

5–10 green Thai, serrano, or cayenne chiles, stems removed

4 tablespoons (59 mL) ground cumin

1 heaping tablespoon (20 mL) red chile powder

1 heaping tablespoon (20 mL) garam masala

2 teaspoon (10 mL) turmeric powder

1 tablespoon (15 mL) sea salt

1. Put the spinach, onion, tomato, ginger, garlic, green chiles, cumin, red chile powder, *garam masala*, and turmeric in the slow cooker. (You can keep the spinach stems on, as it will all be blended later. I also just wash and throw the garlic cloves in without trimming their ends.)

2. Cook on high for 3 hours. Stir once or twice and push down any spinach leaves that stick to the sides so they don't dry out. (At this point, the spinach will be wilted and greenish brown. Don't worry; it will liven up and look much better when you blend it.)

3. Blend until smooth with an immersion blender, or transfer to a blender and do the same. Make sure the large chunks of ginger are broken down. Return the puree to the slow cooker.

4. Add the sea salt and cook on low for another 2 hours. Although the dish may already look done, this last 2 hours of cooking allows the spices to finish cooking and blend better into the dish.

5. After cooking, add about 12 ounces (340 g) cubed fresh or fried *paneer*. Turn off the slow cooker, replace the lid, and let sit for 10 minutes. If you are using homemade *paneer* that is very soft, add it just before serving, as it can dissolve into the spinach if you let it sit too long. Serve with *roti* or *naan*.

You can halve recipe and still safely make it in a slow cooker as large as 5 quarts. You'll end up with 5 cups (1.18 L), including the cheese. I find this dish works better when prepared in larger amounts.

Paneer

*P*aneer isn't complicated to make and worth the effort, because when you make it yourself you can use organic and/or low-fat milk, if you prefer.

4 cups (946 mL) milk (whole, low-fat, or skim)

3 tablespoons (45 mL) fresh lemon juice

1. In a heavy medium saucepan, bring the milk to a boil over medium-high heat. Be careful not to let it boil too fast, as it could boil over. If you let it simmer over too low of a heat, it could collect and burn at the bottom of the pan. The boiling process should take just a few minutes.

2. Remove the pan from the heat and immediately add the lemon juice. Mix well and then cover the pan tightly. Let it sit for at least 10 minutes. Pour the mixture into a large colander lined with cheesecloth. Pull the cheesecloth together at the corners, tie the ends together, and hang the sac above your sink for a few hours. Alternatively, you can use a slotted spoon to scrape the cheese off the top of the pan. Put this cheese on a flat plate, put another plate on top (so the bottom touches the cheese), and put a heavy saucepan on top of that. Let sit for at least an hour.

3. Cut the cheese into 1-inch (2.5 cm) cubes. Use as is, or fry until golden brown.

If you prefer, you can substitute cubed, firm tofu either fresh or fried.

Saucy Punjabi Potatoes

Rase Wale Aloo | SLOW COOKER SIZE: **5-QUART** • COOKING TIME: **9 HOURS ON HIGH** • YIELD: **10 CUPS (2.37 L)**

This recipe is a favorite weekend lunch item. The key is to chop the potatoes into large chunks and cook them long enough that about half of them break down to thicken up the stew. The tomato adds tartness and the chiles provide just enough heat. The recipe took me several attempts to perfect. I finally realized that the simpler I kept the spices, the better it turns out. You want to end up with a dish that is bright with the yellowness of the potatoes and turmeric and the redness of the tomatoes.

The perfect accompaniment is a stack of fried *puris*. Yes, the dish is heavy in carbs, but it's well worth the splurge. If you don't use the potatoes immediately after chopping them, submerge them in cold water to prevent them from turning brown.

3–4 large russet, Yukon Gold, or red potatoes, washed, peeled, and chopped (about 8 cups/1.89 L)

1 medium yellow or red onion, peeled and quartered

1 (2-inch [5 cm]) piece ginger, peeled

2–4 large cloves garlic, peeled

4–6 Thai, serrano, or cayenne chiles, stems removed

2 medium tomatoes

1 tablespoon (15 mL) cumin seeds

1 tablespoon (15 mL) turmeric powder

1 teaspoon–1 tablespoon (5–15 mL) red chile powder

6 cups (1.42 L) water

1 tablespoon (15 mL) sea salt

1 handful, fresh cilantro, chopped

½ cup (125 mL) plain yogurt (optional)

1. Put the potatoes in the slow cooker.

2. In a food processor, grind the onion, ginger, garlic, and chiles. Add this mixture to the slow cooker.

3. Bring a pot of water to a boil on the stovetop. Cut an X into the non-stem end of each tomato with a sharp knife and add the tomatoes to the boiling water. Cook for about 2 minutes, or until the peel starts to curl back. Pull the tomatoes out of the water with tongs, allow them to cool, and peel them. Roughly chop the tomatoes. Add them to the slow cooker.

4. Add the cumin, turmeric, red chile powder, and water. (My mother-in-law insists on the extra turmeric to give the dish a beautiful yellow color.) Cook on high for 9 hours.

5. Using a large serving spoon, mash some of the potatoes against the wall of the slow cooker. This will thicken the broth and create a creamier soup.

6. Add the sea salt, cilantro, and yogurt (if using). Serve with Indian bread (fried *puris* are ideal), spicy *achaar*, and an onion salad.

To make this dish in a 3½-quart slow cooker, halve all the ingredients and proceed with the recipe. A half recipe makes 5 cups (1.18 L).

Ginger-Garlic Eggplant

SLOW COOKER SIZE: **4- OR 5-QUART** • COOKING TIME: **5 HOURS ON LOW** • YIELD: **7 CUPS (1.66L)**

My husband is not a big eggplant fan, so he was apprehensive about trying this dish. Once he did, though, he ate it for a week straight. He went out one night for a work dinner and said that while eating steak he was thinking of how he preferred this eggplant dish. If I can make a convert of him, I'm sure I can make one of you, too. Give it a try and see how many times you make it again!

3 medium eggplants, unpeeled, cut into cubes (about 12 cups/2.5 kg)

2 medium yellow or red onions, peeled and finely chopped

1 (4-inch [10 cm]) piece ginger, peeled and grated or finely chopped

12 cloves garlic, peeled and finely chopped

6–8 green Thai, serrano, or cayenne chiles, stems removed, chopped

1 heaping tablespoon (20 mL) cumin seeds

1 heaping tablespoon (20 mL) red chile powder

1 tablespoon (15 mL) sea salt

1 teaspoon (5 mL) turmeric powder

¼ cup (59 mL) vegetable or canola oil

1. Put all ingredients except the oil into the slow cooker. Drizzle the oil over everything and mix thoroughly.

2. Cook on low for 5 hours. If the eggplant begins to look dry while cooking, just drizzle a little more oil into the slow cooker.

3. Eat with *roti, naan,* or rice.

To make this dish in a 3½-quart slow cooker, halve all the ingredients and proceed with the recipe. A half recipe makes 4 cups (946 mL).

Chickpea Flour Curry with Vegetables

Punjabi Khardi | SLOW COOKER SIZE: **5-QUART** • COOKING TIME: **5 HOURS ON HIGH** • YIELD: **12 CUPS (2.84 L)**

Most regions in India have their own version of *khardi*. The basic ingredients—chickpea flour and yogurt—are the same, but the other ingredients vary depending on where you are from in India and how the dish is prepared in your household.

This dish is not to be mistaken with the term *curry*, which is used incorrectly in the West to refer to most Indian dishes with broth. Traditionally, *khardi* is made with fried vegetable dumplings. To make things less complicated, I just load mine up with a variety of veggies. You can use any combination of vegetables you like along with the onion and cauliflower—such as eggplant, cabbage, bell peppers, okra, or squash. Use a total of about 4 cups [946 mL] veggies. This dish makes a perfect weekend lunch.

½ cup (100 g) chickpea flour (besan)

4 cups (946 mL) plain yogurt or buttermilk

2 cups (473 mL) water

1 tablespoon (15 mL) turmeric powder

1 (4-inch [10 cm]) piece ginger, peeled and coarsely chopped

10 cloves garlic, peeled

2 tablespoons (30 mL) vegetable or canola oil

1 pinch asafetida

1 teaspoon (5 mL) fenugreek seeds

1 large yellow or red onion, peeled and chopped

½ head cauliflower, chopped

1 medium tomato, coarsely chopped

4–8 green Thai, serrano, or cayenne chiles, stems removed

1 tablespoon (15 mL) red chile powder

2 cups (473 mL) water, boiling

1 tablespoon (15 mL) sea salt

1 handful spinach, chopped roughly

1. Put chickpea flour, yogurt or buttermilk, water, and turmeric in a blender and combine well. The result will look like a bright yellow, frothy milkshake. Pour the mixture into the slow cooker.

2. In a food processor, grind the ginger and garlic into a paste.

3. Heat the oil in a shallow pan over medium-high heat. Once it's hot, add the asafetida and fenugreek seeds. When the seeds sizzle, add the ginger/garlic puree and sauté for about 2 minutes, allowing the mixture to brown. It will stick to the pan a bit; just continue to scrape the bottom and sides of the pan to prevent burning.

4. Add the onion and cauliflower to the pan. Cook for a few minutes, until the veggies are soft. Add this mixture to slow cooker. Toss in the tomato, green chiles, and red chile powder.

5. Add the boiling water and sea salt to the slow cooker. Cook on high for 5 hours.

6. Before serving, add the spinach. Let it sit for a few minutes, and then serve over basmati rice.

To make this dish in a 3½-quart slow cooker, halve all the ingredients and proceed with the recipe. A half recipe makes 6 cups (1.42 L).

Fiery Eggplant

SLOW COOKER SIZE: **4- OR 5-QUART** • COOKING TIME: **4 HOURS ON HIGH, 3 HOURS ON LOW** • YIELD: **6 CUPS (1.42 L)**

Inspired by a recipe in one of my favorite cookbooks, *A Little Taste... of India*, I was amazed that I was able to recreate this in a slow cooker. The dish has an amazing taste and uses a unique blend of spices, including fennel and nigella seeds. The result is unlike anything you've tasted before.

15 small eggplants, washed and cut in wedges

3 medium tomatoes

1 (2-inch [5 cm]) piece ginger, peeled and cut in large pieces

10 cloves garlic, peeled

⅔ cup (158 mL) plus 1 tablespoon (15 mL) vegetable or canola oil

1 tablespoon (15 mL) fennel seeds

1 teaspoon (5 mL) nigella seeds (kalonji)

8–10 green Thai, serrano, or cayenne chiles, stems removed, chopped

2 tablespoons (30 mL) ground coriander

1 teaspoon (5 mL) turmeric powder

2 teaspoons (10 mL) red chile powder

1 tablespoon (15 mL) sea salt

1. Place the cut eggplant in a colander, sprinkle with sea salt, and let them stand about 30 minutes to let any bitter juices run out. Rinse, squeeze out any excess water, and pat dry with a paper towel. Place in the slow cooker.

2. Bring a pot of water to a boil on the stovetop. Cut an X into the non-stem end of each tomato with a sharp knife and add the tomatoes to the boiling water. Cook for about 2 minutes, or until the peel starts to curl back. Pull the tomatoes out of the water with tongs, allow them to cool, and peel them.

3. In a food processor, puree 1 tomato, the ginger, and the garlic. Add the puree to the slow cooker.

4. Warm 1 tablespoon (15 mL) of the oil over medium-high heat in a shallow pan. Once it's hot, add the fennel and nigella. Cover the pan and allow the seeds to pop for a few seconds. Scrape them, with the oil, into the slow cooker.

5. Chop the remaining 2 tomatoes and put them along with the green chiles, coriander, turmeric, red chile powder, and the remaining ⅔ cup oil in the slow cooker. Cook on high for 4 hours. Turn the slow cooker to low and cook for 3 hours.

6. Add the sea salt. Enjoy with *roti* or *naan* and a side of onions.

To make this dish in a 3½-quart slow cooker, halve all the ingredients and proceed with the recipe. A half recipe makes 3 cups (710 mL).

Your Notes …

Meats

"When my husband tried my slow-cooked
Nihari, his eyes grew dark and emotional.
He said it reminded him of times with old,
good friends eating the dish after a late
night of partying."

Traditional Chicken Curry

Traditional Chicken Curry

SLOW COOKER SIZE: **5-QUART** • COOKING TIME: **8 HOURS ON LOW** • YIELD: **6-8 SERVINGS**

When most people think of Indian food, the first dish that comes to mind is a good chicken curry. Because I never ate this dish growing up, I relied on my husband's childhood version for this recipe. He says the best chicken curry is made with a rich sauce and no vegetables. Though many recipes call for chopped cauliflower or carrots, I've tried to remain true to his tastes for this recipe.

3 pounds (1.36 kg) skinless whole chicken, cut in about 8 pieces including the breast, legs, and wings (boneless can also be used)

1 large or 2 medium yellow or red onions, peeled and chopped into 8 pieces

2 medium tomatoes, quartered

1 (4-inch [10 cm]) piece ginger, peeled and chopped into 1-inch (2.5 cm) pieces

10 cloves garlic, peeled

1 tablespoon (15 mL) sea salt

1 tablespoon (15 mL) turmeric

1 tablespoon (15 mL) garam masala

¼ cup (59 mL) vegetable or canola oil

1 cup (237 mL) plain yogurt

1 tablespoon (15 mL) red chile powder

½ cup (100 g) dried methi leaves (optional)

1 (2–4 inch [5–10 cm]) cinnamon stick

4 green cardamom pods

4 cloves

4–6 green Thai, serrano, or cayenne chiles, stems removed, halved lengthwise

½ cup (118 mL) boiling water (optional)

½ cup (100 g) fresh cilantro, chopped

1. Put the chicken in the slow cooker. (If the meat was frozen, make sure it is thoroughly defrosted. Never use frozen foods in a slow cooker, because it takes too long to raise the heat to an appropriate level for safe, bacteria-free cooking.)

2. In a food processor, grind the onion, tomato, ginger, and garlic until smooth. This may take a few minutes, so be patient. You want the paste to be as smooth as possible.

3. Transfer the paste to a bowl. Whisk in the sea salt, turmeric, garam masala, oil, yogurt, red chile powder, and methi. Pour this mixture over the chicken.

4. Add the cinnamon stick, cardamom pods, cloves, and green chiles. Mix gently.

5. Cook on low for 8 hours. If you want more broth with your chicken add the water toward the end of the cooking time. Remove the whole spices.

6. Garnish with cilantro and serve over bed of basmati or brown rice or with roti or naan.

Try This! For you vegetarians out there, substitute seitan for the chicken and follow the same steps. Although seitan does not need to cook as long as the chicken would, stick to the cooking time given. The masala still needs to cook thoroughly. If you are concerned that the seitan may get tough, add it in after four hours of cooking.

To make this dish in a 3½-quart slow cooker, halve all the ingredients and proceed with the recipe. A half recipe makes 3 to 5 servings.

Chicken Tikka Masala

SLOW COOKER SIZE: **5-QUART**   •   COOKING TIME: **AT LEAST 2 HOURS TO MARINATE, THEN 6 TO 8 HOURS ON HIGH**   •   YIELD: **14 CUPS (3.31 L)**

There are many theories for how this dish came about. One is that a Bangladeshi-British chef in the United Kingdom came up with the idea to add tomatoes and cream to the original tandoor-cooked chicken and *masala*. Regardless, the popularity of chicken *tikka masala* in the West, especially in Great Britain, is indisputable.

I modified the recipe for the slow cooker and eliminated the step of first grilling the chicken. It still tastes great. If you prefer, grill the chicken before adding it. But try it my way first—you may just find you like it and don't want to bother with the extra step.

Chicken:

2 cups (473 mL) plain yogurt

3 tablespoons (44 mL) lemon juice

1 (1-inch [2.5 cm]) piece ginger, peeled and grated

5 cloves garlic, peeled and grated

1 tablespoon (15 mL) paprika

1 teaspoon –1 tablespoon (5–15 mL) red chile powder

2 teaspoons (10 mL) ground cinnamon

2 teaspoons (10 mL) black pepper

2 teaspoons (10 mL) sea salt

3 pounds (1.36 kg) boneless, skinless chicken, cut into 2-inch pieces

1. Whisk together all the ingredients except the chicken in a deep mixing bowl. Add the chicken and mix gently until all the pieces are coated.

2. Cover and refrigerate at least 2 hours, or, ideally, overnight.

Masala:

6 medium tomatoes

3 medium yellow or red onions, peeled and cut into large pieces

6 cloves garlic, peeled

4–6 green Thai, serrano, or cayenne chiles, stems removed

2 (6 oz [50 g]) cans tomato paste

2 tablespoons (30 mL) garam masala

2 tablespoons (30 mL) ground coriander

1 tablespoon (15 mL) red chile powder

1 tablespoon (15 mL) sea salt

1 tablespoon (15 mL) brown sugar

3 tablespoons (44 mL) blanched sliced almonds (optional)

1 teaspoon (5 mL) ground cinnamon

½ cup (125 mL) water

6 cardamom pods, crushed slightly in a mortar and pestle

1 cup (250 mL) heavy cream

1 cup (201 g) chopped fresh cilantro

Chopped onions, for garnish

Chopped green chiles, for garnish

Chicken Tikka Masala (continued)

1. Bring a pot of water to a boil on the stovetop. Cut an X into the non-stem end of each tomato with a sharp knife and add the tomatoes to the boiling water. Cook for about 2 minutes, or until the peel starts to curl back. Pull the tomatoes out of the water with tongs, allow them to cool, and peel them. Roughly chop the tomatoes.

2. In a food processor grind the onions, garlic, green chiles, tomato paste, *garam masala*, coriander, red chile powder, sea salt, brown sugar, almonds, cinnamon, and water until completely smooth. Be patient, as this might take 5–10 minutes. Stop and scrape down the sides as needed.

3. Add the tomatoes to the food processor and pulse a few times until they break down but are not completely blended. Put this mixture in the slow cooker, along with the crushed cardamom pods.

4. Using a slotted spoon or tongs, slowly add the marinated chicken to the slow cooker.

Discard the remaining marinade to make a thicker base for the chicken, or add it to the slow cooker for a thinner *masala*.

5. Cook on high for 6 to 8 hours. If you want an even thicker sauce, remove the lid an hour before the cooking time ends.

6. Add the cream and cilantro. Garnish with the chopped onions and green chiles. Serve with *roti* or *naan*.

Try This! If you want to add another layer of flavor to the dish, brown the marinated chicken in oil on the stovetop before adding it to the slow cooker. You can also grill the chicken after marinating and serve it with toothpicks as an appetizer.

To make this dish in a 3½-quart slow cooker, halve all the ingredients and proceed with the recipe. A half recipe makes 7 cups (1.66 L).

Butter Chicken

Murg Makhani | SLOW COOKER SIZE: **5-QUART** • COOKING TIME: **6 HOURS ON LOW** • YIELD: **13 CUPS (3.08 L)**

Butter chicken is one of those dishes that have become synonymous with Indian food outside of India. I personally never ate it growing up. In fact, until I got married and we started ordering more takeout from local Indian restaurants, I hadn't even tasted the dish. Regardless, who can say no to butter anything?

After much research, I found that there are many ways to make butter chicken. Some recipes call for the chicken to be pan-fried in butter before putting it into the sauce. Some call for cashews instead of almonds. I went with a recipe in one of my favorite Indian cookbooks, *A Little Taste of… India*, and adapted it for the slow cooker.

If you make this dish and wonder why it doesn't really look like the butter chicken you eat in most restaurants, congratulations, you've made it correctly! Most mainstream Indian restaurants serve *tandoori* chicken smothered in butter and cream as a poor substitute. On top of this, they add unhealthy food dyes for color. I won't lie; this recipe includes butter and cream, but the other fresh and healthy ingredients in this dish make up for the extra calories. However, if you don't like the idea of all this butter or cream, you can cut the butter down to a tablespoon or two and eliminate the cream altogether.

---

8 tablespoons (118 mL) ghee or unsalted butter

4 pounds (2 kg) boneless, skinless chicken breasts and/or thighs

1 (4-inch [10 cm]) piece fresh ginger, peeled and chopped into 1-inch (2.5 cm) cubes

8 cloves garlic, peeled

1 cup (201 g) blanched sliced almonds

½ cup (118 mL) water

2 large onions, peeled and thinly sliced

1½ cups (355 mL) plain yogurt

2 teaspoons (10 mL) red chile powder

1 teaspoon (5 mL) ground cloves

1 teaspoon (5 mL) ground cinnamon

2 teaspoons (10 mL) garam masala

8 green cardamom pods, lightly crushed in a mortar and pestle

2 tablespoons (30 mL) sea salt

5 medium tomatoes, chopped

½–1 cup (100–201 g) chopped fresh cilantro

½ cup (118 mL) heavy cream or half-and-half

Chopped onions, for garnish

Chopped green chiles, for garnish

1. Turn slow cooker to high and add the *ghee* or butter. Cook for 20 to 25 minutes, until it melts.

2. Meanwhile, wash the chicken and cut it into 2½-inch (7 cm) strips. Don't cut it too small, or it will dry out while cooking. (If you are using frozen chicken, be sure to defrost it completely before using it.) Put the chicken in a bowl and set aside.

3. In a food processor, grind the ginger, garlic, and almonds until smooth. Pour in the water and puree to a thick, almost creamy paste. Stop and scrape down the sides as needed.

Butter Chicken (continued)

4. Add onions to the melted butter or *ghee* in the slow cooker and lightly fry for 15 minutes, stirring once or twice. The onions won't brown as they would on a stovetop, but that's okay. Just soften them in the butter. The slow cooker will do the rest later.

5. While the onions are cooking, put the ginger/garlic/almond paste, yogurt, red chile powder, cloves, cinnamon, *garam masala*, cardamom, and sea salt in a bowl and whisk together. Gently fold in the tomatoes.

6. Pour this mixture over the chicken and mix well. Turn slow cooker to low and add the chicken. Cook for 6 hours.

7. Stir in the cilantro and cream. Top with chopped onions and green chiles. Serve with basmati rice or thick *naan*.

Try This! Once the dish is cooked, you can blend it into a soup, chicken and all. If you don't like chunky vegetables, blend the onions and the tomatoes with the ginger, garlic, and almonds for an even smoother, more vibrantly colored curry.

To make this dish in a 3½-quart slow cooker, halve all the ingredients and proceed with the recipe. A half recipe makes 6 cups (1.42 L).

Chicken Vindaloo

SLOW COOKER SIZE: **5-QUART** • COOKING TIME: **7 HOURS ON HIGH** • YIELD: **13 CUPS (3.08 L)**

This dish originated in Goa, and its use of vinegar—and originally, pork—is a clear indication of its Portuguese roots. Known for its spiciness, *vindaloo* is now made with anything, including chicken, beef, lamb, and prawns. Vegetables such as mushrooms and potatoes can also be added, but they are not used traditionally.

2 tablespoons vegetable or canola oil, plus another 2 for frying

8 large yellow or red onions, peeled and thinly sliced

6 tablespoons (89 mL) white wine vinegar

1 (8-inch [20 cm]) piece ginger, peeled and cut into chunks

20 cloves garlic, peeled

6–10 green and red Thai, serrano, or cayenne chiles, stems removed

1 tablespoon (15 mL) turmeric powder

1 tablespoon (15 mL) ground coriander

1 tablespoon (15 mL) garam masala

1 teaspoon (5 mL) ground cinnamon

1 tablespoon (15 mL) black peppercorns

1 heaping tablespoon (20 mL) rock salt

1 tablespoon (15 mL) black mustard seeds

4 pounds (2 kg) boneless, skinless chicken breasts and/or thighs, cut in 1-inch (2.5 cm) pieces

½ cup (125 mL) water

1. Warm the oil in a shallow frying pan over medium-high heat and fry the onions until brown and almost caramelized, about 4 minutes. Be careful not to burn. Add the vinegar and cook, stirring, until the liquid evaporates, about 2 minutes longer. Remove the onions from oil and puree in a food processor along with 2 tablespoons of fresh oil. Set aside.

2. In a food processor, puree the ginger, garlic, green chiles, turmeric, coriander, *garam masala*, and cinnamon. Set aside.

3. In a mortar and pestle, grind the peppercorns, salt, and mustard seeds together into a powder.

4. Put the chicken, onion puree, ginger puree, and peppercorn mixture in the slow cooker. Add the water and cook on high for 7 hours. Serve with fresh *roti* or *naan* or basmati, or brown rice.

To make this dish in a 3½-quart slow cooker, halve all the ingredients and proceed with the recipe. A half recipe makes 6 cups (1.42 L).

Minced Lamb with Peas

Keema | SLOW COOKER SIZE: **5-QUART** • COOKING TIME: **7 HOURS ON HIGH** • YIELD: **10 CUPS (2.37 L)**

My husband was adamant that this dish would not work in the slow cooker. "Are you kidding me? And on top of it you're not going to brown the meat? It will never come out." What he hasn't figured out in 10 years of marriage is that the moment you say the word "never" to me, I find a way to do it. That's what happened with surfing, hula dancing, and now *keema* in a slow cooker.

Follow this recipe, and your guests will never guess you didn't slave over a hot stove all day long!

4 pounds (2 kg) minced lamb

½ cup (118 mL) vegetable or canola oil

1 yellow or red onion, peeled and roughly chopped

1 (4-inch [10 cm]) piece ginger, peeled and cubed

20 cloves garlic, peeled

4–6 green Thai, serrano, or cayenne chiles, stems removed

1 (16-ounce [360 g]) can tomato puree

8 fresh or dried Indian or regular bay leaves

4 tablespoons (50 g) ground cumin

4 tablespoons (50 g) ground coriander

2 tablespoons (30 mL) garam masala

2 tablespoons (30 mL) red chile powder

2 tablespoons (30 mL) sea salt

1 teaspoon (5 mL) turmeric powder

½ cup (100 g) chopped fresh cilantro

2 cups (402 g) fresh or frozen peas

1. Turn slow cooker to high and add the lamb and oil. Allow it to heat up while you prep the other ingredients.

2. In a food processor, grind the onion, ginger, garlic, and green chiles into a paste. Add this mixture to the slow cooker, along with the tomato puree, bay leaves, cumin, coriander, *garam masala*, red chile powder, sea salt, and turmeric.

3. Cook on high for 7 hours. Turn the slow cooker off and add the cilantro and peas. (If the peas are fresh, cook them in boiling water for about 3 minutes before adding.) Replace the cover and let sit for 10 minutes.

4. Eat with steaming basmati rice and fresh onions on the side.

Try This! If red meat isn't your thing, substitute minced turkey or chicken.

To make this dish in a 3½-quart slow cooker, halve all the ingredients and proceed with the recipe. A half recipe makes 5 cups (1.18 L).

Spiced Crumbles with Peas

Mock Keema | SLOW COOKER SIZE: **5-QUART** • COOKING TIME: **3 HOURS ON HIGH** • YIELD: **12 CUPS (2.84 L)**

This dish may be called mock *keema*, but there's nothing to laugh about here. It is absolutely incredible and a great way for vegetarians to enjoy the amazing taste and consistency of traditional keema, which is made with lamb.

I tried this recipe a few different ways, and found it can be made with either non-meat, non-soy alternatives such as Quorn or meatless soy crumbles such as those made by Boca or Morningstar (I prefer the Boca soy crumbles). Use the ones that come in bags in the freezer section of most grocery stores.

The only complaint I've heard about this dish is that it's not greasy enough. Traditional *keema* is made more delicious by the fatty oil the meat gives off while cooking. It's classic comfort food—kind of like eating New York–style thin-crust pizza with oil dripping off each slice. Feel free to add a little more oil in the end if you need it.

If you've never had vegetarian crumbles, this is a great introduction.

4 (12-ounce [340 g]) bags meatless grounds (such as those made by Quorn, Boca, and Morningstar)

½ cup (100 g) vegetable or canola oil

1 yellow or red onion, peeled and finely chopped

1 (4-inch [10 cm]) piece ginger, peeled and cubed

16 cloves garlic, peeled

4–6 green Thai, serrano, or cayenne chiles, stems removed

1 (6-ounce [260 g]) can tomato puree

2 cups (473 mL) boiling water

¼ teaspoon (1 mL) cardamom seeds or 3–4 green cardamom pods, lightly crushed

6 fresh or dry Indian or regular bay leaves

4 tablespoons (50 g) ground cumin

4 tablespoons (50 g) ground coriander

2 heaping tablespoons (40 mL) red chile powder

2 tablespoons (30 mL) sea salt

2 teaspoons (10 mL) turmeric powder

2 teaspoons (10 mL) garam masala

½ cup (100 g) chopped fresh cilantro

2 cups (402 g) fresh or frozen peas

1. If the grounds are frozen, defrost completely.

2. Turn the slow cooker to high. Put the defrosted crumbles, oil, and onion in the slow cooker and mix well. Allow to heat while you prep other ingredients.

3. In a food processor, grind the ginger, garlic, and green chiles. Add this mixture to the slow cooker.

4. Put the tomato puree into a bowl and add the boiling water. Carefully whisk until the paste dissolves. Add this mixture to the slow cooker along with the crushed cardamom seeds or pods, bay leaves, cumin, coriander, red chile powder, sea salt, turmeric, and *garam masala*. Mix well.

5. Cook on high for 3 hours.

6. Add the cilantro and peas. If the peas are fresh, cook them in boiling water for about 3 minutes before adding. You can add frozen peas without boiling them, but let the dish sit for about 10 minutes before serving to warm them up. Eat over basmati or brown rice with chopped, fresh onions on top. If you need a more comfort, drizzle a little more oil over the top.

Try This! James, one of my most loyal taste testers, suggests taking large button mushrooms, cutting away the stems, and stuffing them with mock *keema*. Sprinkle some spicy cheese over the top and bake the stuffed mushrooms in the oven at 375 degrees for about 15 minutes. You can also use this "meat" in tacos.

To make this dish in a 3½-quart slow cooker, halve all the ingredients and proceed with the recipe. A half recipe makes 6 cups (1.42 L).

Lamb Biryani

SLOW COOKER SIZE: **4- OR 5-QUART MEDIUM** • COOKING TIME: **AT LEAST 2 HOURS TO MARINATE, 3 HOURS ON LOW** • YIELD: **8 CUPS (1.89 L)**

*B*iryani is a spiced rice and meat dish that is wildly popular in Pakistan. Muslim travelers and merchants brought it to the Indian subcontinent. Though I didn't grow up eating this dish, my husband frequently ate it after nights out drinking.

The first time I made lamb *biryani*, I immediately thought of shepherd's pie and that this is the South Asian version of that dish, with rice replacing the potatoes. The combination of rice, meat, and vegetables in one makes this dish comforting, delicious, and convenient.

1 (4 inch [10 cm]) piece ginger, peeled and grated

4 garlic cloves, peeled and grated

4–6 green Thai, serrano, or cayenne chiles, stems removed

2 tablespoons (30 mL) garam masala

1 teaspoon (5 mL) red chile powder

1 teaspoon (5 mL) turmeric powder

1 teaspoon (5 mL) sea salt

⅔ cup (120 g) chopped fresh cilantro

¼ cup (50 g) fresh mint, chopped

2 pounds (1 kg) boneless lamb leg or shoulder, cut into 1-inch (3 cm) cubes

1 cup (250 ml) plain yogurt

3 medium yellow or red onions, peeled and very thinly sliced

4 tablespoons (59 mL) canola or vegetable oil

1½ cups (375 mL) water

2½ cups (526 g) uncooked basmati rice

1 tablespoon (15 mL) sea salt

½ teaspoon (2.5 mL) saffron strands, soaked in 2 tablespoons (30 mL) milk (optional)

1. In a deep bowl, mix together the ginger, garlic, green chiles, *garam masala*, red chile powder, turmeric, 1 teaspoon of sea salt, cilantro, and mint. Add the lamb and mix to coat. Marinate at least 2 hours in the refrigerator or, ideally, overnight.

2. After marinating, add the yogurt to the lamb and mix well.

3. Turn the slow cooker on low. Add the onions, 2 tablespoons (30 mL) of the oil, and the marinated lamb to the slow cooker. Cook for 2 hours.

4. On the stovetop, bring the water to a boil over medium-high heat. Add the rice and the tablespoon of sea salt and turn the heat to low. Allow the rice to simmer for 3 to 5 minutes, at which point most of the water will have evaporated. If it has not, use a slotted spoon to transfer the rice to the slow cooker. Discard any remaining water. Level the rice in the slow cooker with the back of a spoon. Drizzle the rice with the remaining oil and the saffron/milk mixture, if desired.

5. Cook for 1 hour, occasionally fluffing the rice with a fork. Scoop and serve this amazing one-pot meal.

Try This! To add another layer of flavor to the dish, brown the onions in oil on the stovetop before adding them to the slow cooker.

To make this dish in a 3½-quart slow cooker, halve all the ingredients and proceed with the recipe. A half recipe makes 4 cups (946 mL).

Pakistani "Old Clothes" Beef Curry

Nihari | SLOW COOKER SIZE: **5-QUART** • COOKING TIME: **9 HOURS ON LOW** • YIELD: **10 CUPS (2.37 L)**

Nihari is a traditional Pakistani dish made from beef. A Mexican-American friend dubbed it "old clothes" curry because he says it resembles a Cuban dish where the beef falls apart just like old clothes.

Making this traditional stew in a slow cooker made total sense, but no one I knew had tried making it this way. When my husband had his first bowl, his eyes grew dark and emotional. He said it reminded him of times with old, good friends, eating *nihari* after a late night of partying. Wow! What an endorsement!

2 medium yellow onions, peeled and sliced

2 pounds (1 kg) beef brisket, trimmed of fat

1 (2-inch [5 cm]) piece ginger, peeled and cut into chunks

10 cloves garlic, peeled

1 heaping teaspoon (7 mL) ground ginger

4 green or white cardamom pods

3 fresh or dried Indian or regular bay leaves

1 (4-inch [10 cm]) cinnamon stick

1 tablespoon (15 mL) garam masala

2 tablespoons (30 mL) ground fennel

1 tablespoon (15 mL) red chile powder

2 pinches ground nutmeg

1 teaspoon (5 mL) turmeric powder

1 teaspoon (5 mL) white salt

1 teaspoon (5 mL) black salt

½ cup (118 mL) vegetable or canola oil

1. Put the onions in the slow cooker. Add the beef.

2. In a food processor, grind the ginger and garlic to a paste and add it to the slow cooker.

3. Add the ground ginger, cardamom pods, bay leaves, cinnamon stick, *garam masala*, fennel, red chile powder, ground nutmeg, turmeric, white salt, and black salt. Drizzle the oil over everything. There's no need to mix.

4. Cook on low for 9 hours. The dish is done when the beef starts to fall apart easily, just like old clothes. Enjoy with thick *naan* and a side salad of onions.

To make this dish in a 3½-quart slow cooker, halve all the ingredients and proceed with the recipe. A half recipe makes 5 cups (1.18L).

Sides, Desserts, & More

"The *Kheer* I ate growing up was simply milk, rice, cardamom, raisins, and sugar cooked on the stovetop until just right. The slow cooker makes the process that much easier."

Rice Pudding

Wet Curry

For those who are not Indian, this dish will take some explanation. *Masala* just refers to mixed spices. *Gila* means "wet." Put them together and you have the base for any curried dish. Most Indian mothers toil over the stove for hours on the weekend preparing *gila masala*. Why? Because it's like having soup broth on hand—you can pull it out of the fridge, mix it with peas and *paneer* or chicken, and prepare an amazing tasting dish in minutes. For my wedding, my mother had a friend make four huge tubs of this *masala* to last us through a week's worth of festivities and family visits.

The *masala* usually takes hours of browning onions on the stovetop and cooking the tomatoes, ginger, and garlic just right to ensure the perfect consistency. My mother never thought it would be possible to make it in the slow cooker. Thank god for my wonderful mother-in-law. She saved the day and made it incredibly easy for me to make the complicated dishes I grew up eating and loving.

3 pounds (1.5 kg) yellow onions, peeled and chopped

1 pound (500 g) tomatoes

5 teaspoons (25 mL) turmeric powder

½ pound (250 g) ginger, peeled and chopped

24 cloves garlic, peeled

2 tablespoons plus 2 teaspoons (39.4 mL) sea salt

½ cup (118 mL) vegetable or canola oil

1. Put everything in the slow cooker, adding the oil last.

2. Cook on high for 4 hours. Puree with an immersion blender or transfer to a traditional blender, puree, and return to the slow cooker.

3. Cook the blended mixture on high for another 8 hours. The longer cooking time is essential to make sure the flavors blend well. The mixture should thicken and bubble as it cooks.

This mix will last 2 to 3 weeks in the fridge. In the freezer, it will last up to 3 months. Use about a cup of this masala in any wet dish on the stovetop from peas and *paneer* (*matar paneer*) to meat curries. You can even experiment in the slow cooker: Just add veggies and this *masala* and cook on low for a few hours.

Try This! Double or triple the amount of tomatoes for more of a tomato base.

I don't recommend making this in the 3-quart slow cooker, because it defeats the purpose of making a large amount to keep on hand.

Mango Chutney

Aam kee Chutney | SLOW COOKER SIZE: **3½-QUART** • COOKING TIME: **6 HOURS ON HIGH** • YIELD: **2 CUPS**

I never really ate mango chutney before I started making it in the slow cooker. Now, I can't get enough of it. It's super easy to make and such a great side to Indian and non-Indian dishes. It will keep in your fridge for weeks at a time.

5 ripe mangoes, peeled, pitted, and chopped (about 3 cups)

1 (2-inch [5 cm]) piece ginger, peeled and grated or pureed

4 cloves garlic, peeled and minced or grated

1 (3-inch [6.5 cm]) cinnamon stick

6 cloves

1 teaspoon (5 mL) red chile powder

⅜ cup (90 mL) white vinegar

½ cup (110 g) brown sugar

1. Put everything in the slow cooker and mix well.

2. Cook on high for 6 hours, until the whole mixture thickens. Serve on the side of Indian dishes.

Try this! Serve alongside grilled meats like chicken or lamb. Or do as my buddy James does—mix this chutney with rice for a low-calorie treat. Heat it and eat in place of dessert.

Homemade Yogurt

Dhai | SLOW COOKER SIZE: **5-QUART** • COOKING TIME: **13½ HOURS TOTAL, ON LOW AND WITH THE COOKER TURNED OFF** • YIELD: **8 CUPS (1.89 L)**

Indians love their yogurt. I'm not talking about the heavy, creamy, and overly sweet dessert type of yogurt that's popular in the West. I mean a lighter, tangier, homemade variety that's mixed with spices and grated veggies like cucumbers, carrots, and onions and served as a side with dinner.

My mother still has the small, opaque glass cups that fit into her home-made yogurt machine when I was a little girl. These days, she uses them as stand-in drink glasses. After all, who has time to make yogurt at home? Well, now you do!

My hunch that this could be done was reaffirmed through research and a recipe from fellow slow cooker–book author Stephanie O'Dea. Make this once, and you'll never go back to the more expensive store-bought variety.

8 cups milk (1.89 L) (whole, low-fat, or skim; do not use ultra-pasteurized)

½ cup (125 mL) natural, live/active-culture plain yogurt

1 thick bath towel or blanket

1. Put the milk in the slow cooker and turn it on low. Cook for 2½ hours.

2. Unplug the slow cooker, and let it sit for 3 hours with the cover on.

3. After 3 hours, transfer 2 cups (473 mL) of the lukewarm milk to a bowl and whisk in the live/active-culture yogurt. (This is basically any plain yogurt you have leftover—either previously homemade yogurt or a store-bought version.) Keep in mind that the yogurt you make will take on the taste and quality of the culture you are using, so don't use a batch that is older or sour—which I made the mistake of doing the first time. If you know an Indian family, ask them for a sample of their culture, which will likely be better than anything bought from the store.

4. Put the mixture back in the slow cooker and stir gently.

5. Replace the lid and wrap the towel or blanket around the slow cooker to keep the contents warm. Let it sit, still unplugged, for 8 hours. Enjoy blended with fruit or with chopped veggies and sea salt and pepper. This also makes a wonderful base for *lassi*, an Indian yogurt-based drink.

To make this dish in a 3½-quart slow cooker, halve all the ingredients and proceed with the recipe. A half recipe makes 5 cups (1.18 L).

Rice Pudding

Kheer | SLOW COOKER SIZE: **5-QUART** • COOKING TIME: **3 HOURS ON HIGH** • YIELD: **9 CUPS (2.13 L)**

There's something universal and comforting about rice pudding, and *kheer* is no exception. It's the perfect Indian dessert because it's not overly sweet or syrupy, especially spiced with a little cardamom and sweetened with golden raisins.

I have seen this recipe in other cookbooks made with ingredients like evaporated milk and toasted pistachios, but the *kheer* I ate growing up never had such complications. In our house, it was simply milk, rice, cardamom, raisins, and sugar cooked on the stovetop until just right. The slow cooker just makes the process that much easier. Now my family can enjoy it every week.

1 teaspoon (5 mL) vegetable or canola oil

1 cup (201 g) white basmati rice, washed thoroughly

¼–½ cup (59–118 mL) sugar or agave nectar

1 teaspoon (5 mL) seeds of green cardamom, lightly crushed

½ cup (118 mL) golden raisins

8 cups (1.89 L) milk (whole, low-fat, skim, or unsweetened soy)

2 tablespoons (30 mL) finely chopped slivered almonds or pistachios

1. Coat the bottom and sides of slow cooker with a thin layer of oil.

2. Put the rice, sugar, cardamom, raisins, and milk in the slow cooker. If you are using agave nectar, I recommend adding it toward the end, as adding it early makes the dish pinkish-brown in color. It will be delicious either way.

3. Cook on high for 3 hours, stirring once or twice. Be careful not to let it overcook, or the milk will separate. If there is any browned milk caked on the sides, just scrape it out with a spoon and discard before serving.

4. Sprinkle chopped almonds or pistachios across the top, and serve hot or cold.

To make this dish in a 3½-quart slow cooker, halve all the ingredients and proceed with the recipe. A half recipe makes 5 cups (1.18 L).

Carrot Halwa

Gajar Halwa **or** *Gajrela* | SLOW COOKER: **5-QUART** • COOKING TIME: **9 HOURS ON HIGH** • YIELD: **7 CUPS (1.66 L)**

Growing up, I remember my mother spending all day cooking this dessert on the stovetop. The pot would rattle, sometimes the milk would boil over, and she'd constantly have to adjust the heat. The slow cooker makes the process so much easier. The only real work is grating the carrots, and take my word—doing it by hand is well worth the effort.

Served hot or cold, this is a delicious and nutritious dessert.

2 pounds (1.2 kg) carrots, peeled and washed thoroughly

6 cups (1.42 L) whole milk

2 cups (402 g) sugar

1 cup (201 g) raw almonds, crushed or chopped

½ cup (118 mL) melted ghee or butter

½ cup (100 g) golden raisins

½ teaspoon (2 mL) ground cardamom

1 tablespoon (15 mL) ground pistachios

1 tablespoon (15 mL) ground almonds

1. Grate the carrots by hand. (This dish is a labor of love, and this is the labor. The carrots break down much better if they are hand grated. Alternately, you can grate them in a food processor. I've found that store-bought grated carrots are not worth using because they are too thick and too long.) Put the carrots in the slow cooker.

2. Bring the milk to a boil on the stovetop and pour it over the carrots in the slow cooker.

3. Cook for 3 hours on high. Remove the slow cooker lid and cook for another 3 hours on high. Replace the lid, but leave it slightly open and cook on high for 3 more hours. By now, the carrots will be cooked and will look soft and watery.

4. Transfer the carrot mixture to a wide, heavy pan and cook on the stovetop on medium-high for 15 minutes.

5. Add the sugar and continue cooking, stirring, for another 15 minutes. While stirring, slowly add the crushed almonds and the *ghee* or butter. Add the raisins and ground cardamom and continue stirring.

6. When the carrot mixture pulls away from the sides of the pan on its own and becomes thicker, it's done. Take the pan off the heat and let the mixture cool for about 15 minutes.

7. Garnish with the ground pistachio and almonds.

To make this dish in a 3½-quart slow cooker, halve all the ingredients and proceed with the recipe. A half recipe makes 4 cups (946 L).

Essential Sides

Rice: The key to making fluffy rice is to get the proportion between the rice and water right. For white rice, including basmati, use double the amount of water. So, for 1 cup (201 g) rice, use 2 cups (591 mL) water. For brown rice, use double plus an extra cup of water. So, for 1 cup (201 g) brown rice, use 3 cups (708 mL) water.

To add an Indian touch to the rice, heat 1 tablespoon oil over medium-high and add about half a medium onion sliced, 2 cloves, 2 large black cardamom pods, and a stick of cinnamon. Brown the onions slightly and add a cup of rice, 2 teaspoons of sea salt, and 2 cups of water. Cover the pan with a lid, making sure to leave it open a bit to let the steam out. Cook for about 20 minutes, until the water evaporates.

Roti/Naan: *Naan* can be found in most grocery stores, while *roti*, also called *chapati* or *phulka*, is more readily available at an Indian grocer. Keep in mind that *roti* is the healthiest option, as it's made with whole-wheat flour. *Naan* can also be healthy if you purchase a whole-wheat version.

To make my own *roti*, I usually mix the dough in my food processor. The proportion that works best for me is 3 cups (603 g) *aata* to 1½ cups (354 mL) water and 1 tablespoon vegetable or canola oil. I blend the mixture until it becomes a sticky ball, much like pizza dough. Then I knead it on my clean countertop, which has been prepped with a thin layer of dry *aata*. Pull off small balls, about 2 inches in diameter, dip them into dry *aata*, and roll them out with a rolling pin into thin circles. Cook on a preheated, flat frying pan until browned on both sides. Stack the *rotis* as you finish cooking them. They'll keep in the fridge for about a week. Use chapati 100% percent whole-wheat flour from an Indian grocery store for the best results.

Yogurt/raita: Indians generally eat plain, savory yogurt. To add some basic Indian touches, add a pinch each of sea salt, black salt, and red chile pepper to a cup of plain yogurt and serve it with your Indian meal.

To make a *raita*, follow the same instructions, but also add anything from grated cucumber, to chopped onions and tomatoes, to pomegranate seeds. Anything is possible, and the more you experiment, the more variations you'll come up with.

Chutneys: Mint chutney is probably the most common Indian chutney. To make it, take a large bunch of mint leaves, remove and discard the hard stems, and grind them in a blender or food processor with a small piece of peeled ginger, 2 cloves garlic, a small chopped onion, 2 small green chiles, sea salt, red chile powder, and a little lemon juice. To jazz it up a bit, substitute fresh cilantro for half the mint leaves.

Indian Onion Salads are my passion. I have to have raw, fresh onions with my meal or I don't feel like I've actually eaten. For a basic salad, put sliced raw onions, sliced cucumbers, and sliced tomatoes on a large plate. Sprinkle with sea salt, black salt, and red chile powder. Squeeze half a lemon over the top and serve.

Paneer, or homemade Indian cheese, is similar to ricotta. It's not too difficult to make as long as you have a little patience and the right tools. Heat 4 cups (946 mL) of whole or low-fat milk over medium-high heat just until it starts to boil. Add 3 tablespoons of fresh lemon juice. Cover the pot and let it sit for about 15 minutes. Skim the cheese off the top into a layer of cheesecloth or muslin that is layered into a colander placed over a plate. Once much of the water drains away, gather the sides of the cheesecloth together and twist them together to create a sack. Lay the sack on a plate, put another plate on top, and add something heavy to weigh it down. Let it sit for an hour to squeeze the water out. Chop the *paneer* into chunks and use.

Burnt Onions: Finely chop 1 large yellow or red onion. Heat 3 tablespoons vegetable or canola oil in a frying pan over medium-high heat. Stirring occasionally, cook until the onions are dark brown. Sprinkle over dishes before serving. This topping can last in the fridge for up to 2 weeks. They will soften a bit but will still be delicious as a topping to any dish.

Your Notes ...

Index

About the Author

ANUPY SINGLA was a television reporter for Chicago-based and Tribune-owned CLTV for years before giving it all up to cook. She was determined to learn how to make every Indian recipe she grew up with, from sweet to savory, in a quest to reconnect with her Indian roots and teach her young daughters to appreciate wholesome and healthy Indian food. She blogs about her experiences at www.indianasapplepie.com. Her food-related writing has appeared in the *Chicago Sun-Times*, the *Chicago Tribune* and the *Wall Street Journal*. Anupy is an award-winning journalist who has also reported for Bloomberg News and WGN-TV. She has a masters in Asian Studies from the East West Center and the University of Hawaii, and also worked on Capitol Hill as a legislative aide. She cooks and writes from her Lincoln Park home in downtown Chicago, where she also teaches kid and adult cooking classes and tries to perfect her Hindi, Japanese, and French.